scrapbook page|maps

sketches for creative layouts
beckyfleck

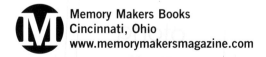

Memory Makers Books
Cincinnati, Ohio
www.memorymakersmagazine.com

acknowledgments

To my mom, Susan, who has steadfastly believed in me, even when I didn't believe in myself. You have been an extraordinary parent and friend.

To Linda, who shares in all my triumphs, both great and small. I couldn't be more appreciative of your encouragement.

To Fred, who may not get the whole scrapbooking thing, but tries to get excited anyway. Dude, I think this is the closest I'm going to get to *The Carol Duvall Show*!

To my editors, Christine Doyle and Amy Glander, who would never admit how silly some of my questions were. Thank you for your infinite patience.

To Tricia, whose kickin' photography helped me design many of the layouts in this book. Thanks for letting me rent those cute kids, girl.

To the divine Miss M, Little D, Judi, Tiff, Mindy, Pat-tay, Ames, Grill, Sheredian, Vicki, Becky, Sweet Tart, Kim and Connie—all of you rocked the sketches of this book.

To all the fans and friends of PageMaps—you have inspired me beyond measure.

Finally, to my wonderful, supportive husband, Chris, who stopped asking, "What's for dinner?" about halfway through the writing of this book. I so owe you a home-cooked meal. I love you, Colonel.

In loving memory of Pam Drumheiser.

Thanks for the nudge, my friend, and hold the door open for me.

Scrapbook Page Maps Copyright © 2008 by Becky Fleck. Manufactured in China. All rights reserved. It is permissible for the purchaser to make the projects contained herein and sell them at fairs, bazaars and craft shows. No other part of this book may be reproduced in any form or by any electronic or mechanical means including information storage and retrieval systems without permission in writing from the publisher, except by a reviewer, who may quote a brief passage in review. Published by Memory Makers Books, an imprint of F+W Publications, Inc., 4700 East Galbraith Road, Cincinnati, Ohio 45236. (800) 289-0963. First edition.

12 11 10 09 08   5 4 3 2

Distributed in Canada by Fraser Direct
100 Armstrong Avenue
Georgetown, ON, Canada L7G 5S4
Tel: (905) 877-4411
Distributed in the U.K. and Europe by David & Charles
Brunel House, Newton Abbot, Devon, TQ12 4PU, England
Tel: (+44) 1626 323200, Fax: (+44) 1626 323319
E-mail: postmaster@davidandcharles.co.uk
Distributed in Australia by Capricorn Link
P.O. Box 704, S. Windsor, NSW 2756 Australia
Tel: (02) 4577-3555

Library of Congress Cataloging-in-Publication Data
Fleck, Becky
  Scrapbook page maps : sketches for creative layouts / Becky Fleck. -- 1st ed.
      p. cm.
  Includes index.
  ISBN 978-1-59963-016-8 (hardcover/case/plc/wire-o : alk. paper)
  1. Photograph albums. 2. Scrapbooks. I. Memory Makers Books. II. Title.
TR501.F58 2008
745.593--dc22

                              2007043493

Editor: Amy Glander
Designers: Karla Baker, Corrie Shaffeld, Jeremy Werling
Art Coordinator: Eileen Aber
Production Coordinator: Matt Wagner
Photographer: Melanie Warner; Adam Henry, Alias Imaging LLC
Stylist: Nora Martini

www.fwpublications.com

Me, at three years old, holding my first trout.

firstsketches

Over the past four years, I can't tell you how many times someone has asked me, "When are you going to write a sketch book, Fleck?" or "How did you get started creating sketches?" I always met the first question with a shake of my head and a nifty eye roll, but a reply to the second question always makes me smile. The whole sketching thing got started all because of football. Yes, football.

I am a die-hard Minnesota Vikings fan. I'd practically lay down my life for the purple and gold. One football weekend, several years ago, I got to thinking about a few layouts I needed to finish that coming week, and began doodling a few sketches on a piece of paper while watching the game. Over several weekends, my small collection of sketches grew and I shared them with my online friends. One Sunday, I was watching a particularly exciting game between the Vikings and their arch nemesis, the Green Bay Packers, and ended up with a rather large set of sketches. I posted them online Monday morning and my bud, Shawna (a Packer fan, although I forgive her for it), commented that I'd had a rather prolific weekend in the sketch department. She asked, "What's up with that?" to which I sarcastically replied, "Silly girl, the Packers lost." And so I started the ritual of creating sketches during football season.

When I'm not designing, sketching, scrapbooking or watching football, you'll find me standing in water, waving a stick. I fly fish from April to October with my husband and our three furry retrievers, Jackson, Hannah and Darby. (To digress for a moment, has anyone happened to notice how lucky my husband is to have found me? I mean come on, I love football and fishing! Sorry, but I just had to point that out.) I also enjoy camping, a bit of gardening and any book written by Dean Koontz. Chris and I live on an old cattle ranch near the Yellowstone River in southeast Montana, where it is truly the "last, best place."

S'U

ph

2.5"

I love the opportun
Alex and Grace. They
that "it" factor wher
mug shots. Amy had
photos for her holid
wanted to wear her
the shoot. My initia
way!" But I agreed
cooperated for th
would do so
when we
photos

LAUGH

consideri
far from
so desper
as. And it is
neighbor girls [whe
cats and dogs] get
a few minutes in
time Amy looks at
see Alex and Gra
two sisters who
much and can alw

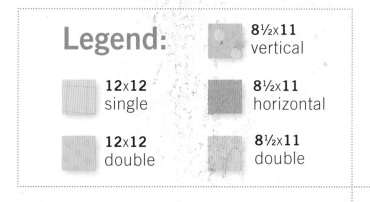

Legend:

8½x11 vertical

12x12 single

8½x11 horizontal

12x12 double

8½x11 double

photo

5.5" x 2.5"

CLASSIFIED

any given sunday

confessions of a foo a

CALIFORNIA GOLDEN BEARS

ARIZONA STATE SUN DEVILS

VIKINGS

MINN

KC

SUNDAY SUNDAY SUNDAY SUNDA

photo

3.25" x 2.5"

Have you ever found yourself staring at a pile of photos, a few sheets of patterned paper and some cool embellishments, and say to yourself, "Now what?" Hitting a creative wall is like stubbing your toe in the middle of the night—the pain is temporary, but oh-so annoying. When my scrapbooking mojo takes a hiatus, I rely on sketches to jump-start my creativity. A quick flip through my sketch book and suddenly the muse is back in the house.

In this book I'm joined by 14 incredibly talented artists (five contributors and nine Friends of PageMaps) who have widely diverse and distinct styles. As you turn the pages of this book, I hope you will be inspired by the exceptionally inventive and creative interpretations of 60 different sketches in five popular sizes. Useful artist tips, step-by-step instructions and Eye Spy's are scattered throughout each chapter, offering extra pointers and ideas to try.

As an added bonus, there is a handy, ready-to-assemble deck of cards at the end of the book. These cards include all 60 sketches, plus a sample layout and alternate supply lists, conveniently color coded by size. Once assembled, this card deck can easily slip into your supply bag to take to crops and scrapbook events, or you can even tuck it into your purse when you shop at your local scrapbook store. Heck, you can even play Go Fish with them!

Whether you are just getting started in scrapbooking or you've been addicted for years, this book is sure to spark your imagination. May you always find pleasure and satisfaction in this wonderful hobby we all call scrapbooking.

Here's to creativity,

Becky

You are the author of your life's adventure. Weave your tales of wonder, save a place to dream, and believe in your brave heart. **Unknown**

"One can never consent to creep when one feels an impulse to soa[r]"
Helen Ke[ller]

When I read this quote, I knew it was meant for you. I remember when you [...]
your 3-year check up with Dr. Taoka. She said you reminded her of Helen Ke[ller...]
Helen Keller was incredibly determined, very intelligent, and sensitive and, [...]
tially, became easily frustrated because of her inability to communicate. A [...]
these traits remind me so much of you. You have [...]
ated your own language and learned to communica[te ...]
other non-verbal ways. As the years have passed, yo[u ...]
gradually learning everything you have always kno[w...]
your mind but haven't been able to say. I admire [...]
strength and determination and I hope that one [...]
of your struggles will be a distant memory.

soa[r]

I know that once you learn how to com[municate]
verbally, you will become a different pers[on...]
years are just the beginning of a lifetime [...]
for you, Kylie. I hope each and every day [...]
tinue to feel the impulse to soar, just [...]
Keller did. I will be here for you every [...]
way and don't ever give up baby girl.

photo
2.25" x 3"

using sketches and making them your own

I love to cook. As an only child, I grew up in a household comprised mainly of women, so my culinary endeavors started at a very young age. There are certain recipes I will follow to the letter (altering them met with disastrous results!), while others are more adaptable, offering me a chance to swap ingredients depending on what I have on hand.

Imagine, for a moment, that a sketch is like your favorite recipe. You bring all the ingredients together (photos, journaling, paper and embellishments) and follow the sketch like cooking instructions. Yet, as you create a layout, you may add or skip an ingredient, try an innovative technique, move an element around, or add just the right amount of spice to create an entirely new design.

A sketch serves as a basic visual template, and whether you follow a sketch to the last detail or draw inspiration from a specific element, it is your imagination and ingenuity that will create a unique layout that transcends your personal style.

> Imagination is the beginning of creation. You imagine what you desire, you will what you imagine and, at last, you create what you will. **George Bernard Shaw**

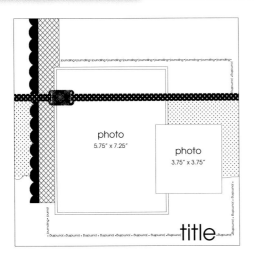

photo
5.75" x 7.25"

photo
3.75" x 3.75"

title

At first glance of this sketch, you might ask, "Where's the journaling?" Upon closer inspection, you'll see a continuous stream of text that parades around the photos and intersects the title. In my layout, the journaling is further enhanced with a single sewing stitch inside the imaginary box. A small brad placed at each corner where the text makes a right-hand turn squares up the design. Printing continuous journaling like this takes some practice and patience, but the results are definitely unique and different. See Judi and Marla's layouts on the next page to see how they added their own special twist to this technique.

Supplies: Cardstock (Bazzill); acrylic paint, metal frame, patterned paper, ribbon, stickers (Making Memories); chipboard numbers and symbol, rub-ons (BasicGrey); silk flower (Heidi Swapp); crackle accent (Ranger); chalk (Pebbles); mini brads (Queen & Co.); adhesive (3M, Glue Dots); thread; JakeOpti Antique font (Internet download)

Photo: Amy Goldstein

eye spy

Did you notice the blue paint spatters on the white silk flower? It really makes the petals pop!

Marla devised yet another creative solution to the wrap-around journaling on this sketch, where she used letter stickers to tell the story of her son Liam's "twisty" habit. An assortment of ribbons tied onto a wire circle make a perfect embellishment and strategically placed, hand-cut arrows draw the eye to the subject of the page.

Supplies: Cardstock (Prism); die cuts, patterned paper, rub-ons (Sassafras Lass); chipboard letters (BasicGrey); letter stickers (American Crafts, BasicGrey); ribbon (Strano); acrylic paint (Making Memories); adhesive (3M)

Artwork: Marla Kress

y it with me now: "Retro funk-ay!" I really dig this lay-
ut and the way Judi approached the journaling square
n the sketch. Bypassing the direct-to-paper method,
e printed her journaling on a transparency and then
t it into strips. This technique takes the hassle out
squaring up the journaling to the elements on the
age. The rest of her uninhibited design comes together
th capricious elements (check out those circa 1970s
b-ons) and lots of sparkly bling, creating energy and
otion. Someone bust out the disco ball!

pplies: Cardstock (Bazzill, Prism); patterned paper (Imagination
ject, Mustard Moon, Upsy Daisy); chipboard letters (Imagination
ject); transparency; chipboard (Fancy Pants); rub-ons (Fancy
nts, K&Co.); glitter chipboard heart (Melissa Frances); ink (Nick
ntock, VersaMark); brads (Bazzill); dimensional glitter, glossy
cents (Ranger); stamps (Purple Onion); embossing powder (Jo-Ann);
hesive (Henkel, Therm O Web); Misproject font (Internet download)

work: Judi VanValkinburgh

tip: Black-and-white photo conversions are easy to do in image-editing software, and they can make an otherwise unusable photo scrap-worthy. When Judi took the photo in "Date Night," the blue tint of her windshield obscured the top half of the photo. By converting this photo to black and white and adjusting the contrast, she salvaged an otherwise fantastic shot.

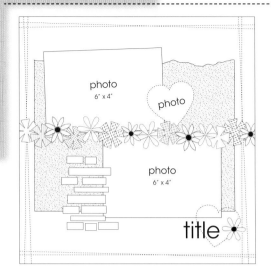

This sketch was perfect to showcase "then and now" photos of my beautiful mom that span more than forty-five years. The authentic journaling strip reveals the many triumphs and hardships in her life. A horizontal row of various-sized, die-cut flowers bisects the two photos, emphasizing the shift in time. A mix of aged and modern-day patterns set a contemporary, yet vintage, mood.

Supplies: Cardstock (Bazzill); patterned paper (Bo-Bunny, Daisy D's, K&Co.); rub-ons (BasicGrey, Daisy D's); die-cut flowers (Provo Craft); transparency (My Mind's Eye); die-cut letters (QuicKutz); corner rounder; distress ink (Ranger); chipboard heart (Cosmo Cricket); adhesive (3M, Glue Dots, KI Memories); Amazone font (Internet download)

tip: Rather than layering papers, one on top of the other, get more mileage from your patterned paper by cutting out a frame and utilizing the unused portion for additional embellishments or other projects.

Although the fuss of cutting up journaling into snippets and segments can be time consuming, it is an ideal solution when you have small chunks of text that do not flow together smoothly. I continued the theme of piece journaling found on the sketch, creating pockets of text around the entire perimeter of the photo. I subtitled the various elements on contrasting cardstock, creating unity with the various tones of green found in the patterned paper and the photo. The lengthy title, constructed from same-size letter stickers, took the place of the two smaller, supporting photos found on the sketch.

Supplies: Cardstock (Bazzill); patterned paper (Crate Paper); sequin flower (Doodlebug); brads (Queen & Co.); letter stickers (BasicGrey); distress ink (Ranger); adhesive (3M, Glue Dots); Milk & Cereal, Prissy Frat Boy fonts (Internet download)

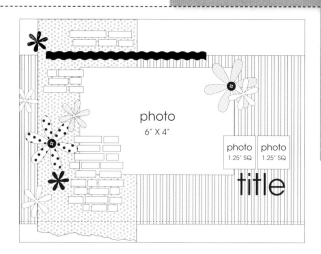

Drawing inspiration from the many embellishments of the sketch, Marla replaced the scattered flowers with bright, bold stars that, contrasted on a black background, seem to shoot right off the page. The tail coming out of the largest star creates motion, drawing the eye toward the main photo. The playful style of her handwritten journaling is visually supported by the photos of her adorable son Liam. Childlike foam letter stickers make for an eye-catching title on this all-boy layout.

Supplies: Cardstock (Bazzill); patterned paper (CherryArte); letter stickers (American Crafts); red cord (unknown); adhesive (3M)

Artwork: Marla Kress

One of the challenges of creating a multi-photo layout is finding harmony in all your photos. This particular sketch lends itself well to solving that problem because the eight supporting photos are quite small in contrast to the large focal photo. Using a sketch like this, you could even get away with blurry, less-than-perfect photos you might not otherwise scrap. With photos as colorful as these, I chose complementary patterned papers that weren't overwhelming. The subtitle is tucked inside a round bookplate, unifying it with the concentric circles of the title.

Supplies: Cardstock (Bazzill); patterned paper (American Crafts, Making Memories, Sassafras Lass); flowers, letter stickers (American Crafts); paper frills (Doodlebug); rub-ons (Heidi Swapp); rickrack (Making Memories); brads (Queen & Co.); chipboard circle trim (Magistical Memories); chipboard bookplate (Beary Patch); decorative scissors; adhesive (3M, Glue Dots); American Standard, Courier Standard font (Microsoft)

tip: Quite by accident, I discovered that when you attach foam flowers to a page using brads, and push the brad firmly, but gently as you pry apart the prongs to secure, it forces the petals of the foam flower to lift up. This technique creates added dimension to your page. Who knew?

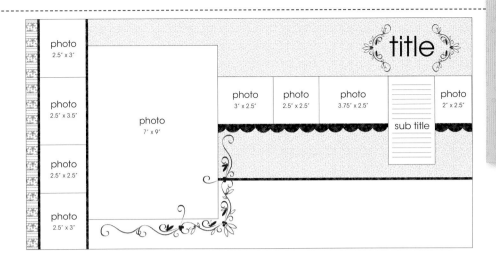

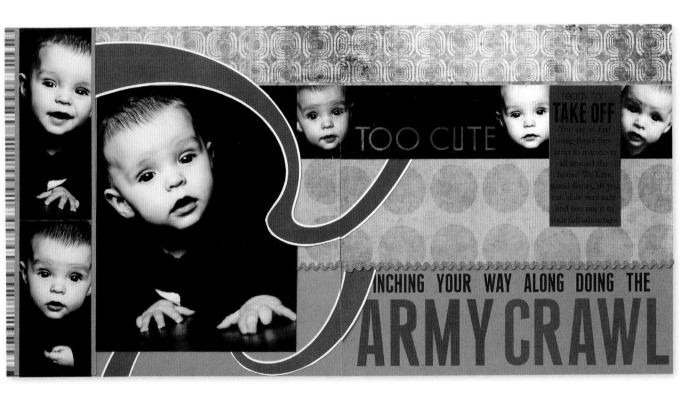

By combining photos, Mindy converted this nine-photo sketch into a six-photo layout, strategically keeping two photos of her adorable son, Aiden, in full color. A thin strip of multi-colored striped paper on the left side drives the color combination for the rest of the page. Flowing ribbons of hand-cut patterned paper convey motion and unify both halves of the double layout.

Supplies: Cardstock (Prism); patterned paper (Bo-Bunny, Dream Street, Upsy Daisy); ribbon (Making Memories); adhesive (Tombow); Garamond font (Microsoft); MLB Astros font (Internet download)

Artwork: Mindy Bush

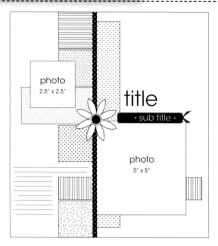

I needed room for a spacious title, and this sketch definitely fit the bill. With an attention-grabbing photo depicting a fence line of brassieres, I played on the "diva" nature of my subject by using a variety of pink patterned papers. (This sketch would work especially well with scraps from your stash.) Although I didn't have a second photo as the sketch depicts, a zoomed and cropped area of the main photo testifies to the fact that they were, indeed, bras strewn about the fence! A bead-filled, acrylic flower is the crowning touch on this girly, hilarious layout.

Supplies: Cardstock (Bazzill); patterned paper (Adornit, KI Memories, Paper Salon, Provo Craft); chipboard letters (EK Success); tag (Pressed Petals); acrylic flower (KI Memories); glossy dimensional medium, ink (Ranger); glass beads (Mill Hill); micro beads (Darice); foam flower (Adornit); rub-on letters (American Crafts); chipboard; die-cut tag (Provo Craft); brads (Queen & Co.); ribbon (Making Memories, Stemma); decorative scissors; adhesive (3M, Glue Dots); Apple Garamond Light font (Internet download)

give it a try

1 — Choose an acrylic embellishment that is flat on one side and inverted on the other, such as a watch crystal, flower or frame.

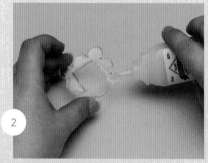

2 — Turn acrylic embellishment over and fill basin halfway with dimensional medium.

3 — Sprinkle glass seed beads into dimensional medium and allow them to sink, followed by micro beads to fill in gaps. Allow to dry overnight.

Denine's no-nonsense approach to this sketch resulted in a lovely, well-adapted layout. A variety of pastel patterned papers play softly against the beautiful baby photos and the entire page is double-matted on white and pink cardstock, grounding all the elements. Small, floral circles attached with tiny brads accent the page in a visual triangle, keeping the focus on the main photo, which rests on an irregularly scalloped frame.

Supplies: Cardstock (Bazzill); patterned paper (BasicGrey, Deja Views, Dream Street); chipboard letters (Li'l Davis); letter stickers (BasicGrey); die-cut circles (Déjà Views); brads (Making Memories); chipboard circle (Technique Tuesday); button (Autumn Leaves); circle punch; adhesive (EK Success, Plaid); Angelina font (Internet download)

Artwork: Denine Zielinski

When scrapbooking vintage photos, there is no rule that says you have to use vintage colors. Although the patterns I chose are reminiscent of age-old prints, the color palette is very modern. After flipping the sketch horizontally, I added snippets of my grandfather's favorite sayings, recessed inside the squares of patterned paper and bulleted with an antique brad to show the beginning and end of each quip. Heart-warming journaling describes a grandfather whom I love and miss.

Supplies: Patterned paper (Autumn Leaves, Flair, K&Co.); letter tabs (Martha Stewart); rub-on letters (American Crafts); word stickers (Creative Imaginations); paper clips, rub-ons (K&Co.); leather medallion (Karen Foster); brads (Making Memories); circle scissor (EK Success); circle punch; adhesive (3M); Nigma font (Internet download)

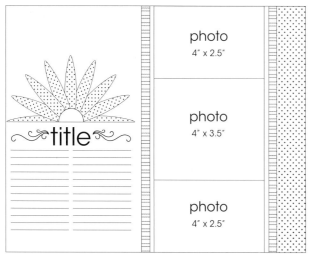

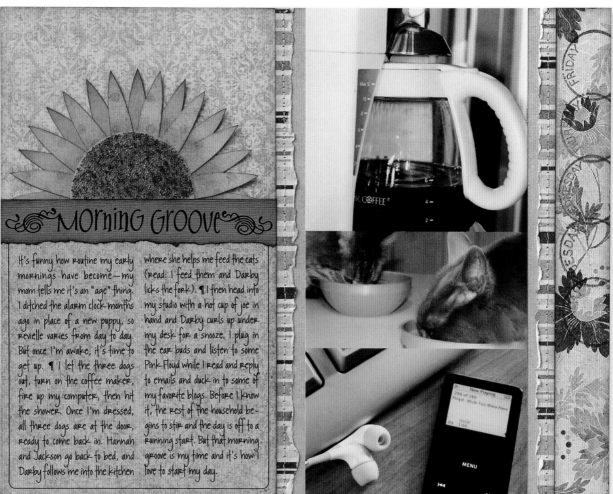

The morning sunrise above the title (which takes the place of the flower found on the sketch) was fashioned with a double layer of patterned paper petals and a half circle of chipboard covered with vibrant micro beads, all resulting in a dimensional punch of color. The lengthy journaling runs together, but is broken up with two paragraph symbols. Three casual photos support the morning drill, and torn paper and a touch of stitching add to the lighthearted theme of the layout.

Supplies: Patterned paper (Bo-Bunny); rub-ons (Cosmo Cricket); glossy accents, distress ink (Ranger); stamps (Purple Onion); micro beads (Magic Scraps); chalk (Pebbles); adhesive (3M, Glue Dots); Rockford font (Internet download)

Judi's first tactic for this sketch was to turn it vertically so she could scrap it in her favorite 8½" x 11" (22cm x 28cm) format. The three stacked photos became two, with a third epoxy photo supporting her clear-lettered title. Judi raided her husband's toolbox and divided the upper photos and lower title area with a piece of electrical tape (how cool!). Directional arrows, label tape journaling and lots of distress ink give this layout a rhythmic, urban feel. (Do the bright orange subway seats remind you of 1970s pop culture? Cue the Bee Gee's soundtrack!)

Supplies: Patterned paper (Imagination Project, Scribble Scrabble); chipboard word (Imagination Project); distress ink (Ranger); epoxy stickers (Creative Imagination); rub-ons (Cactus Pink); label (Dymo); paint pen (Sharpie); adhesive (Henkel, Tombow, Therm O Web); electrical tape

Artwork: Judi VanValkinburgh

There's no telling what a kid will say and this layout captures the essence of my friend Tricia's young son Chase. Because the photos were facing to the right, I decided to flip the sketch horizontally, placing the journaling to the right. The journaling reads like a conversation, capturing word for word the entertaining exchange between Tricia and Chase. Mickey Mouse ears trimmed from cardstock and a sparkling, mixed-letter title foster the playful, amusing theme.

Supplies: Cardstock (Prism); patterned paper (Sweetwater); letter stickers (Making Memories); adhesive (3M); Bernhard Modern, Romantha fonts (Internet downloads)

Photos: Tricia Ribble

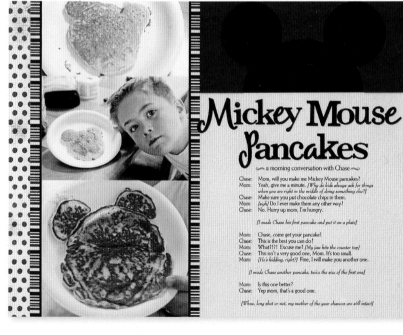

Use a mix of two fonts in conversational journaling to set apart spoken and unspoken dialogue.

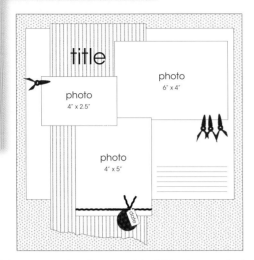

Make no mistake about it: A bold background of black and lime green definitely tells you that this is a dude's page. To support the vertical posture of the photos, I turned the sketch clockwise. The name and location of each New Zealand guide is branded on an oversized photo anchor and the entire page is mounted onto a piece of white cardstock, bringing all the elements together.

Supplies: Cardstock (Prism); patterned paper (Fancy Pants, Sweetwater); rub-ons (American Crafts); brads, grommet (Making Memories); letter stickers (Arctic Frog); chipboard photo anchors (Technique Tuesday); corner rounder; adhesive (3M); ITC American Typewriter font (Microsoft)

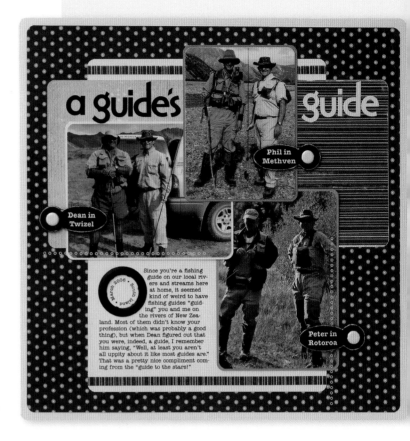

Tiffany's daughter inherited her grandmother's sweet tooth, not to mention her bandit-like traits and this layout unites their love of all things sweet. Humorous strip journaling takes the place of a paragraph, telling the tale of these mischievous, adorable photos. Rounded corners, a whimsical title, and punches of bright blue and orange support the carefree, lighthearted theme of the layout. Now I'm hungry! Cake, anyone?

Supplies: Cardstock (Prism); patterned paper (Arctic Frog, Dream Street, My Mind's Eye); letter stickers, sticker accents (Arctic Frog); circle punch; corner rounder; ink (Ranger); adhesive (3L); Georgia font (Microsoft)

Artwork: Tiffany Tillman

A row of concentric circles serves as the platform to Tiffany's contrasting title on her layout and really makes it pop!

Goofy photo of me holding tickets? Check. Photo of Broadway street sign? Check. Two good friends enjoying a night on the town in Manhattan? Check. In selecting the three photos depicted on this sketch, I scaled the subject of each one at different distances to avoid them merging together. Handwritten journaling tucked around the printed elements of patterned paper, tells the story of my fantastic New York City adventure. After seeing *Mamma Mia*, I had the musical score running through my head for days!

Supplies: Cardstock (Bazzill); patterned paper (Autumn Leaves, My Mind's Eye); transparency (My Mind's Eye); chipboard letters (My Little Shoebox); acrylic paint (Making Memories); brad (Queen & Co.); ink (Ranger); adhesive (3M, KI Memories); pen (Pigma Micron)

tip: If you feel like all the elements of your page are beginning to blend together, try introducing a punch of black for contrast and separation, as I did on this layout above.

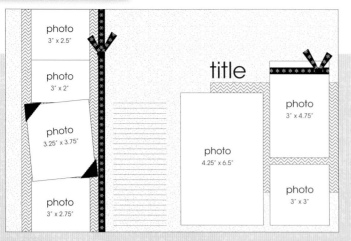

eye spy

Take note of the two colors of gingham ribbon that were used to attach the tags to this page.

The versatility of this sketch is demonstrated in that I used only half of the design to create a single page in a 12" x 12" (30cm x 30cm) format versus the original 8½" x 11" (22cm x 28cm). The mischievous images support the title, and the journaling ends with a dingbat heart—a sweet reminder that Kylie is, undeniably, a little (tom) girl.

Supplies: Cardstock (Bazzill); patterned paper (Heidi Grace); letter stickers (American Crafts, Arctic Frog); ribbon (Doodlebug); chipboard square (Urban Lily); resin sticker (Stemma); silk flowers (Heidi Swapp); adhesive (3M, Glue Dots); Landsdown font (Internet download)

Photos: Tricia Ribble

This 8½" x 11" (22cm x 28cm) double layout that supports eight photos was a great way for Denine to capture all the fun of a trip to the Build-A-Bear store. To help her bright, colorful photos stand out, she trimmed them just a bit beyond the edge to create a white mat around each one. The childlike title gets an added punch with the irregular placement of the letter "F," and the playful theme and palette of youthful colors scream "Fun!"

Supplies: Cardstock (Bazzill); patterned paper (A2Z, Imaginisce); chipboard circle (Scenic Route); brads (Making Memories); letter stickers (American Traditional); rub-on letters (American Crafts); adhesive (EK Success); Decker font (Internet download)

Artwork: Denine Zielinski

A wispy, subtle leaf background and reverse-painted title pull the photos of this page to the front and center. I extended the large focal photo on the sketch to a full, dramatic 12" (30cm) to support the height of the flagpole. To its right, a strip of pleated patterned paper adds a punch of texture and width, leading the eye into the journaling, which is printed on spatter-painted cardstock. Sewing details add to the country charm.

Supplies: Cardstock (Bazzill); patterned paper (Chatterbox, Melissa Frances); mask (Heidi Swapp); letter stickers (Making Memories); acrylic paint (Delta); rub-ons (7gypsies); chipboard tags (BasicGrey); ribbon; thread; adhesive (3M, Glue Dots); Granada SF font (Internet download)

give it a try

1 Spell out the title in an arrangement of letter stickers.

2 Select several colors of acrylic paint that complement your layout. Squirt out a quarter-sized puddle and thin with acrylic thinner or water to an inky consistency.

3 Dip toothbrush into paint and run your thumb over the bristles to spatter paint over the stickers. Multiple applications of each color will achieve the best result.

Allow to dry, then carefully remove letter stickers.

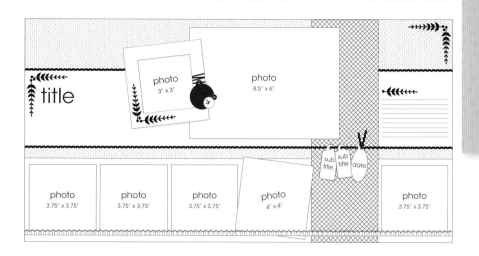

An impromptu nature walk with her daughter Lita turned into a day of fascination and discovery. Tiffany's design stayed true to this seven-photo sketch with a variety of photos that celebrated this special day. Her richly written details of their autumn adventure, tucked around a leaf sticker, express her hope that Lita will come to appreciate the world around her. Fall-themed papers and elements capture the essence of the crisp, cool day, and tiny lettering details are a reminder of how small Lita is in this great big world.

Supplies: Cardstock (Prism, WorldWin); patterned paper (KI Memories); chipboard letters (Scenic Route); chipboard heart (Heidi Swapp); circle punch; letter stickers (EK Success); leaf stickers (Sandylion); brad (Imaginisce); ink (Ranger); adhesive (3L); Serifa BT (Internet download)

Artwork: Tiffany Tillman

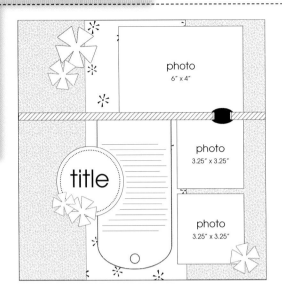

There is nothing more delightful than finding the perfect gift for someone. Although pink garden flamingos all decked out in funky hats and purses might not be for everyone, they certainly tickled my aunt when she opened them for her birthday. The pink theme is central throughout this girly layout with papers, embellishments and a circular title bulleted with pink mini brads. The sketch was flipped horizontally and the two smaller photos were combined into one.

Supplies: Cardstock (Bazzill); patterned paper (Dream Street, Fancy Pants, Scenic Route); embossed cardstock (Doodlebug); letter stickers (American Crafts); mini brads (Queen & Co.); buttons (SEI); paper flowers (Prima); brads, floss, tags (Making Memories); rub-ons (K&Co.); decorative scissors; adhesive (3M); Broadsheet font (Internet download)

Sincere, yet humorous, journaling imparts Connie's devoted affection for her adorable daughter Megan on this love-themed page. Hearts and arrows accent the page in a visual triangle, drawing the eye to the photos. A bold, red title leads into the heartfelt journaling, which is handwritten on a stamped invoice taking the place of the tag depicted on the sketch. What's not to "love" about this layout?

Supplies: Cardstock, patterned paper (Crate Paper, My Mind's Eye); chipboard letters (Heidi Swapp); stamps (Art Declassified); ink (Ranger); ribbon (Wrights); adhesive (3M, Glue Dots, Sailor); thread; pen (Zig)

Artwork: Connie Petertonjes, *Friend of PageMaps*

eye spy

Connie used the negative piece left over from popping the "Y" out of the nested chipboard letter and backed it with patterned paper.

have a magnet on my refrigerator that says, "The trouble with life is . . . it's so daily!" Judi took this adage to heart and created a page about all that happened one particular day. A whimsical row of stamped owls takes the place of the ribbon found on the sketch. With a preprinted journaling block, she listed, in bullet point fashion, random musings of the day. She then recorded a lengthy list of chores and errands she had completed that day around the perimeter of the page.

Supplies: Cardstock (Bazzill); patterned paper (BasicGrey, K&Co.); die-cut tag (Creative Imaginations); letter stickers (American Crafts); rub-on words (Stemma); charm (Bo-Bunny); stamps (Sideshow Stamps); ink (StazOn); sticker (7gypsies); adhesive (Henkel, Therm O Web, Tombow)

Artwork: Judi VanValkinburgh

eye (spy)

A swipe of cream paint into the recesses of the dog bone charm really helped the word "woof" let out a bark!

When my mom sent me this list of a dog's ten pet peeves, I just knew I had to scrap it. As I read each one, I could easily see any one of my dogs sharing those same thoughts (good thing they can't speak!). I must confess that I am a huge offender of number six. To accommodate such a long list and make room for the large title, I turned the sketch 180° and swapped the second photo with the list. Numbered stickers quickly identify each of the ten peeves, and with the help of a heavy-duty hole punch, the suede leather ribbon takes on the guise of a dog collar. Woof!

Supplies: Cardstock (Bazzill); patterned paper (Flair, Melissa Frances, Mustard Moon); chipboard numbers (Cloud 9); letter and number stickers (BasicGrey); dog bone charm, rub-on paw print (Flair); suede ribbon (Karen Foster); thread; Cropadile (We R Memory Keepers); adhesive (3M, Glue Dots); American Typewriter font (Microsoft)

With a classic simplicity that personifies her style, Mindy employed the rule of thirds and created a layout that truly engages the eye. She combined two photos into one and dropped the center photo below the baseline, where it rests atop a band of patterned paper. To make room for the larger foam letter stickers, Mindy placed her journaling above the title. That is one cute kid!

Supplies: Cardstock (American Crafts, Bazzill, Prism); patterned paper, rub-ons (K&Co.); letter stickers (American Crafts); adhesive (Glue Dots, Tombow); Garamond font (Microsoft)

Artwork: Mindy Bush

tip: The "Rule of Thirds" is a design principle that divides space within thirds. Visualize a grid of three horizontal lines and three vertical lines. Place the important elements at one or more of the points at which these lines intersect.

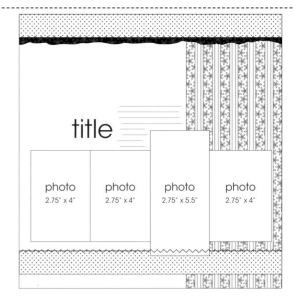

You are almost a year old now! I can't believe how quickly the time has passed! You bring us so much joy and we love to see that cute little smile of yours. We get this grin every single day, sweet, happy and always with your tongue sticking out!

tongue

Although this double sketch supports eight photos, I was able to comfortably squeeze in three more small shots by reducing the size of the photo on the far right. For added interest, I used one image in place of the four small ones on the far left side, quartering the photo after I printed it. Rounding the corners on the right side of each photo provides direction, as your eyes naturally read the layout from left to right. Even though some of the patterned paper is vivid and bright, using it in small, thin strips doesn't overpower the rich, vibrant photos. A wide swatch of cream cardstock spans the middle, giving the photos and journaling a place to casually rest. Isn't that old truck just the coolest?

Supplies: Cardstock (Prism); patterned paper (Autumn Leaves, Scenic Route); stamps (Purple Onion); foam flower (American Crafts); flower stickers (Adornit); rhinestone brads (Making Memories); chipboard tag (BasicGrey); chipboard scrolls (Cactus Pink); ink (Ranger, VersaMark); ribbon (May Arts); decorative scissors; adhesive (3M, Beacon, Glue Dots); Fling, Port Credit fonts (Internet downloads)

The random pattern of a vine-like stamp and a watermark ink pad really brought the blue cardstock background to life.

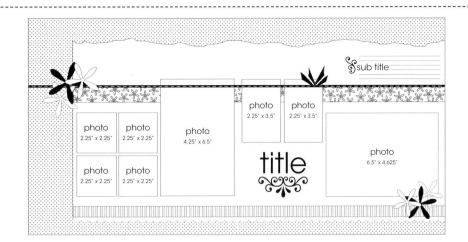

Inspired by her favorite short film *For The Birds*, Dawn created this captivating page full of whimsy and charm. She and her daughter Carly spent a day at Woburn Safari Park where, quite clearly, Carly made some new feathered friends. This eight-photo sketch was perfect for such a great collection of memorable photos. Dawn's unique brand of humor plays throughout the layout as the tiniest of details skip about the page.

Supplies: Cardstock, brads, blossoms, chipboard letters (Bazzill); patterned paper (BasicGrey, Daisy D's, Imaginisce); pearl brads (SEI); ghost flowers (Maya Road); rub-on flowers (Doodlebug); jumbo brad (Heidi Swapp); button; sequins (Mei Flower); stickers (EK Success); ink (Clearsnap); brush pens (Sugarloaf); adhesive (Herma)

Artwork: Dawn Inskip, *Friend of PageMaps*

tip: Choose two same-sized silk flowers in contrasting colors. Cut each in half and rejoin one-half of each color for a unique look.

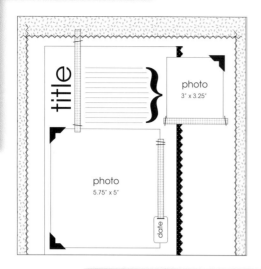

An engaging vertical title placed on horizontally striped patterned paper naturally makes the eye read left to right, but what about the focal photo? Overlapping the title onto the photo quickly solved the problem. All the page elements rest on a body of bright white notebook paper offering contrast and breaking up the frenzied patterned paper beneath it.

Supplies: Cardstock (Bazzill, WorldWin); chipboard shapes, patterned paper (BasicGrey); chipboard letters (Heidi Swapp); rub-ons (Cosmo Cricket, Daisy D's, Martha Stewart, My Mind's Eye); ink (Ranger); decorative scissors; adhesive (3M); staples

tip: Does your title feel a bit blah? Try masking a portion of it with plastic mesh and dabbing a bit of acrylic paint over it in a coordinating color for an instant textured effect.

My friend Tricia's daughter Kylie cannot form many words or complete sentences, yet what she lacks in speech she more than makes up for in tenacity and determination. The epitome of a tomboy, Kylie is a little girl after my heart. The focal photo is placed at an angle to create visual interest, adding movement and energy already reflected in the photo itself. A large, bold title bisects the candid journaling and evocative photos support Tricia's heartfelt thoughts about her daughter's disability.

Supplies: Cardstock (Bazzill, Prism); patterned paper (Prima); chipboard letters (My Little Shôebox); chipboard shapes (Making Memories, Melissa Frances); transparency (My Mind's Eye); hat pin (Heidi Grace); glass beads (Mill Hill); rubber stamps (Purple Onion); chipboard; ink (VersaMark); adhesive (3M, Glue Dots); Bernhard Modern, Tempus Sans fonts (Internet download)

Photos: Tricia Ribble

The intense, saturated rainbow in this photo could be easily overwhelmed if given too much attention with patterned paper, reinforcing the adage that "less is more." Taking the place of the flourishes found on the sketch, thin strips of rainbow colors crown the top of the page, drawing the eye down to the title in invisible vertical lines. Exaggerated rounded corners, diagonally opposite to one another, mimic the arc of the rainbow.

Supplies: Cardstock (Bazzill, Doodlebug, Prism); patterned paper (BasicGrey, KI Memories); circle punch; ink (Ranger); adhesive (3M, Glue Dots); Establo, Gauntlet Classic fonts (Internet downloads)

I absolutely dig everything about this layout, but one of the most clever embellishments has to be the row of trees across the top, secured with a bit of zigzag sewing to create a faux trunk. Following the sketch, Marla carefully selected her focal photo to avoid the title area covering up anything important in the photo. The height and depth of her photo magnify how small her young boy is among a forest of tall trees, adding to the childlike quality of the page. Detailed journaling, housed in a circle of cardstock, shares the magic of Liam's search for the perfect holiday tree.

Supplies: Cardstock (Bazzill); patterned paper (Imagination Project); circle stickers (Memories Complete); date sticker (7gypsies); letter stickers (American Crafts); ribbon; thread; adhesive (3M); Georgia font (Microsoft)

Artwork: Marla Kress

eye spy

Note the small, red pen dots that frame the journaling circle on Marla's layout. This a great alternative to traditional matting.

To better accommodate the width of my photo, I turned this sketch counterclockwise to a horizontal format. A large chipboard flower took the place of the second, smaller photo and a black, mixed-letter title pinch hits in the journaling area. Because the message about my favorite aunt was private, I chose to place it on a tag and tuck it behind the photo. Black photo mats break up the bright, busy colors and patterns, unifying the page.

Supplies: Cardstock (Bazzill); patterned paper (Urban Lily); chipboard letters (Cosmo Cricket); chipboard flower (Maya Road); resin sticker (Stemma); die-cut tag (Provo Craft); brads (Making Memories); acrylic paint (DecoArt); adhesive (3M, Glue Dots); thread; ribbon; Kayleigh font (Internet download)

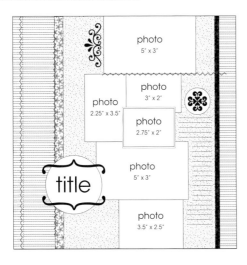

Supplies: Cardstock (Bazzill); patterned paper (A2Z, Making Memories); chipboard letters (Chatterbox); letter stickers (American Crafts); rub-ons (Autumn Leaves, Fancy Pants); floss (DMC); adhesive (3M, EK Success, Glue Dots); feathers; pine needles; Covington font (Internet download)

The collage arrangement of this sketch lent itself well to the subject of my page, but to avoid all the photos blending together, I sanded the edges of each to create an irregular white border. Foam dots lift the lantern photo off the page and the edges of the mat are torn and inked, adding to the rough appeal of the layout. Staying true to my unconventional style brought the outdoors inside, incorporating pine needles and feathers into the title.

It is not difficult to spot the "interloper" in this collage of photos. To avoid a gallery of same-subject photos blending together, I converted all but one to sepia tone. A heart behind the title takes the place of the circle found on the sketch. Detail-rich journaling tells the tale of how one young pup has managed to infuse herself into a well-established pair of littermates, emphasizing her persistence to succeed. Doesn't this page remind you of a *Where's Waldo* book?

Supplies: Patterned paper, chipboard (BasicGrey); rub-on (Martha Stewart); brads (Making Memories); ink (Ranger, VersaMark); pen (American Crafts); thread; ultra thick embossing enamel; adhesive (3M, Glue Dots); Gauntlet Classic font (Internet download)

Select a photo and open it in image-editing software.

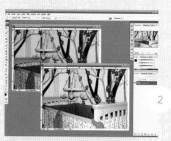

Convert the photo to black and white, print it out, and resave the photo under a new name.

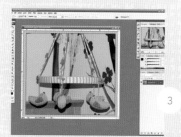

Reopen the color version and isolate and crop the area of the photo you'd like to remain in color. Print the color portion and, using pop dots or dimensional foam adhesive, apply it over the top of the black-and-white photo, lining up the cropped color image with the black-and-white photo beneath it.

...oto collages, as seen in this sketch, can sometimes be tricky because the photos ...ve a tendency to blend together. Marla avoided this issue with some inspiration ...m the hit television show, *Trading Spaces*. Her solution? Convert the photos to ...ack and white, then isolate a portion of the photo in color. Using three colors of ...epe paper, Marla created the beautiful cherry blossom that adorns the top of her ...urnaling. A leftover piece of pom-pom trim from the nursery bedding frames the ...ht side of the page. The urban feel of her layout is right on, with just a touch of ...minine appeal. Can you "dig" it?

...pplies: Cardstock (Bazzill); patterned paper (BasicGrey); letter stickers (American Crafts); adhe-...e (3M, adhesive foam); ball trim; crepe paper

...work: Marla Kress

tip: When using polka-dot patterned paper, add a few random brads to the centers of the dots. I tried this on my "3rd Wheel" layout on page 36 to add some dimension.

oop Dreams

the versatility
of sketches

Sketches provide an infinite amount of design flexibility. For instance, is your photo tall and narrow, but the sketch is drawn to fit a short, wide picture? Try rotating or flipping the design. Do you prefer to scrap in a 12" x 12" (30cm x 30cm) size, but the sketch you'd like to use is in an 8½" x 11" (22cm x 28cm) format? It will convert easily to fit your favorite size. Perhaps you have three great photos, but the sketch calls for five. No worries—photos can be enlarged, reduced or combined. Do you want to create a boy page but the sketch depicts floral embellishments? Ditch the petals and change the design elements to fit your theme.

I encourage you to abandon the notion that you have to follow the sketches of this book exactly as they are drawn. Think with a creative, open mind and freely interpret the sketches with your own distinctive flair. The results will stay true to your personal style.

> The creation of something new is not accomplished by the intellect, but by the play instinct acting from inner necessity. The creative mind plays with the objects it loves. Carl Jung

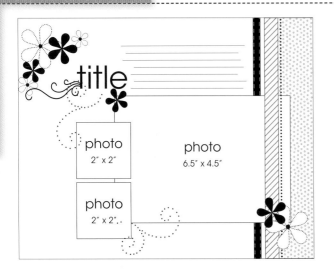

For a little girl who was afraid of the water, "Magic Goggles" were just the ticket to help Kylie overcome her trepidation. The result is a beaming look of pride on her face when she realized she could swim. Replacing the flowers drawn on the sketch, chipboard teardrops covered in aqua blue paper and clear micro beads look like splashes of water, further enhanced with swirly dots of white paint. A thin lead line unites the journaling with the photos, bringing all the elements together.

Supplies: Cardstock (Bazzill); patterned paper (Paper Salon, Three Bugs in a Rug); letter stickers (BasicGrey); chipboard shapes (Fancy Pants); micro beads (Darice); glossy accents, ink (Ranger); acrylic paint (Delta); corner rounder; adhesive (3M); Broadsheet font (Internet download)

Photos: Tricia Ribble

he soft, feminine qualities of this page were achieved ith the use of understated patterned papers and a and-cut script title. I first rotated the sketch vertically accommodate the height of my main photo, and wide, single close-up of the tender lilac blossoms kes the place of the two smaller photos depicted the sketch. Swirly doodles of white painted dots hance the light, airy theme of the page, and small am flowers bloom in random clusters.

upplies: Cardstock (Bazzill); patterned paper (Chatterbox, ggy Tales); Magnetic Precision Mat (BasicGrey); foam flowers merican Crafts); mini brads (Queen & Co.); brads, eyelet trim laking Memories); decorative scissors; chalk (Pebbles); acrylic int (Delta); adhesive (3M, Glue Dots); Broadsheet, Fling fonts nternet download)

The idea of Denine's son Ryan growing up and leaving home is a bit daunting to her and she wanted to share her thoughts about it on a layout. Although this sketch does not make room for lengthy journaling, Denine overcame this space obstacle by continuing her journaling directly onto the main focal photo. A simple title of letter stickers divides the two areas of journaling, breaking it into more readable chunks. Flourishes anchored in opposite corners beautifully frame the layout.

Supplies: Cardstock (Bazzill); pattern paper (Delish Designs); letter stickers (BasicGrey); brads (Making Memories); buttons, die-cut border (My Mind's Eye); ink (Tsukineko); rubber stamps (Autumn Leaves); fabric stiffener (Duncan); adhesive (EK Success, Glue Dots); fabric; AL Uncle Charles font (Internet download)

Artwork: Denine Zielinski

eye spy

Did you notice the irregularity of the lines of type on the top half of the journaling? This disjointed approach emphasizes the emotionally charged journaling.

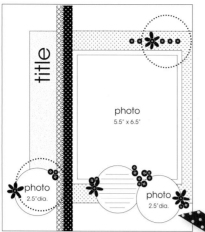

The circles have it in this sketch, but don't limit yourself to this geometric shape when embellishing your page. Mix it up with other shapes, as I did with the floral chipboard frames on my layout. Because I only had the one photo of me and my bud Marla, I replaced the remaining two photos with circular elements. One of them came in quite handy as it lassoed the first word in my title, and the second allowed me to expand the size of my journaling circle so I could yuk it up about my favorite gal pal. A ring of brads at the top right corner "round" out the page.

Supplies: Cardstock, brads (Bazzill); patterned paper (Fancy Pants, SEI); chipboard (Cosmo Cricket); velvet flowers and trim (Maya Road); rub-ons (Crate Paper); buttons (SEI); binder clip, ribbon (Making Memories); "friends" tiny tag (Sweetwater); ink (Ranger); adhesive (3M, Glue Dots); Milk & Cereal font (Internet download)

Photo: Nate Kress

eye spy

Don't be afraid to allow embellishments to fall outside the parameters of your layout. A small binder clip secures the "where and when" of this layout.

Kendall and Grandpa Jim have a very special bond. I love seeing how much they love each other.

July 2005

this is Love

Nothing is more touching than a small child in the arms of her grandpa, and Vicki's captivating layout expresses the love that her daughter Kendall and her Grandpa Jim share. Romantic hues of rosebud pink, pale green and warm brown reinforce the kindhearted theme, and the creamy lace and scattered buttons give the page a vintage, gentle appeal. After a clockwise turn of the sketch, all of Vicki's elements fell into place.

Supplies: Patterned paper (My Mind's Eye); chipboard letters (Heidi Swapp); chipboard swirl (Maya Road); rub-on letters (Anna Griffin); flower punch (Emagination); photo corners (Chatterbox); pen (American Crafts); adhesive (Glue Dots, Hermafix); flower; buttons; kite string

Artwork: Vicki Harvey, *Friend of PageMaps*

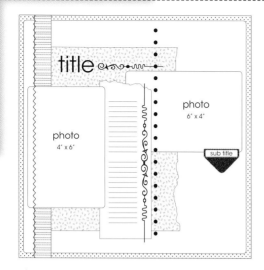

Supplies: Cardstock (Bazzill, Paper Company); patterned paper (Scrapworks); letter stickers (Arctic Frog); plastic star (Heidi Swapp); chipboard arrow (Polar Bear); ink (Ranger); rub-ons (Daisy D's); corner rounder; circle scissor (EK Success); adhesive (3M, Glue Dots); Teen font (Internet download)

Photos: Tricia Ribble

He jumps! He shoots! He scores! This boy's got game! OK, Dick Vitale I'm not, but these powerful, highly contrasted black-and-white photos demanded little more than to be front and center. A bit of black and cream patterned paper, a touch of sewing, and an arc made of black cardstock connecting the left photo with its intended target, brought together this übercool black-and-white page. Yeah, baby!

This "sweet" page expresses the romantic acuity of childhood innocence, combining vintage patterns with contemporary embellishments. An oversized title, intertwined with transparent hearts, connects the two focal photos. A path of tender blossoms stretches horizontally across the center of the page, stopping short of the left side of the photo, and continuing on the right. I rotated the sketch clockwise to better accommodate the orientation of my photos, which I converted to a sepia tone.

Supplies: Cardstock, patterned paper (My Mind's Eye); chipboard letters (Piggy Tales); mini blossoms (Making Memories); letter stickers, rub-ons (BasicGrey); resin photo corner, trim (Melissa Frances); clear heart (Heidi Swapp); pen (Uni); glass beads (Mill Hill); corner rounder; thread; adhesive (3M, Glue Dots); Broadsheet font (Internet download)

Photos: Tricia Ribble

title

photo
2.5" x 3.5"

photo
3" x 3.5"

photo
3" x 3.5"

Tiffany and I were on the same wavelength when it came to the photo area of this sketch, but she took the twist two steps further. First, she converted the sketch to a roomier 12" x 12" (30cm x 30cm) format, and then, in the tri-photo area, she used one panoramic shot of her adorable daughter chasing seagulls. Tiffany's easy-to-read, authentic journaling tells the sweet story of the wide-angle focal photo. Nature-driven embellishments and whimsical pen details complement the outdoor theme of the page.

Supplies: Cardstock (Prism, WorldWin); patterned paper (Arctic Frog); letter stickers (Arctic Frog, EK Success); chipboard letters (Heidi Swapp); rub-ons (Imaginisce, Urban Lily); acrylic paint (Making Memories); adhesive (3L); pen (Zig); Courier T1 font (Internet download)

Artwork: Tiffany Tillman

At first glance, this sketch appears quite girly, but with a bit of swapping and replacing, it quickly morphs into a masculine layout. Besides, my favorite uncle would have my head if a flower appeared on a layout about him! Don't discount the usefulness of a sketch just because it has more photos than you do. That was exactly my dilemma, which I quickly solved by repeating the same photo three times. In image-editing software, I duplicated the photo twice, lightening each one 25% and 50%, then placed masculine brackets on the full-color photo for added emphasis.

Supplies: Cardstock (Bazzill); chipboard brackets, patterned paper, photo corner, small star (Cosmo Cricket); chipboard letters (Crate Paper); chipboard star (My Little Shoebox); ink (Ranger); adhesives (3M, Glue Dots); John Doe font (Internet download)

Because her photos were taken at different times and places, Denine achieved skillful harmony and balance with this sketch by converting all but one of the photos to black and white. Doing so draws focus to a charming color photo of her son Ryan. The hip vernacular of her title is wedged among a row of irregularly shaped squares and stars, taking the place of the floral motif drawn on the sketch. An invoice stamp serves as a great journaling block, cleverly pinch-hitting for one of the photos.

Supplies: Cardstock (Bazzill); patterned paper (Bo-Bunny, Making Memories); die-cut letters, stars (QuicKutz); die-cut squares (Provo Craft); letter stamps (Purple Onion); accent stamps (Art Declassified, Stamps by Judith); ink (Clearsnap); rub-on numbers (BasicGrey); pen (Creative Memories); adhesive, tag (EK Success); Typewriter font (Internet download)

Artwork: Denine Zielinski

eye (spy)

Did you spot the rub-on numbers identifying each photo? These numbers correspond to the journaled list of Ryan's favorite things.

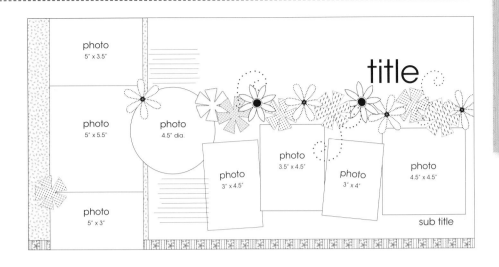

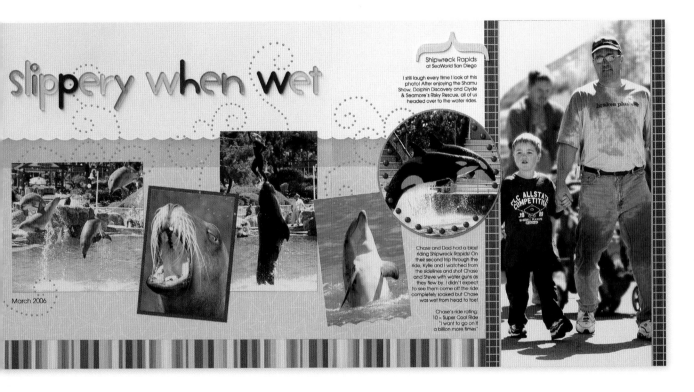

After a quick horizontal flip of the sketch, a series of fantastic marine animal action shots leads into a full-length photo of a happily soaked boy (and his equally wet dad), all chronicling a day at SeaWorld. Swirls of dotted blue paint meander in and out of the title, integrating it with the rest of the page. A palette of bright, youthful colors leaves no doubt that this spring day was drenched in fun!

Supplies: Cardstock (Bazzill, Prism); acrylic letters, patterned paper (KI Memories); brads (Bazzill); chipboard bracket (BasicGrey); acrylic paint (Delta); glossy accents (Ranger); chalk (Stampin' Up); adhesive (3M, KI Memories); AvantGarde font (Microsoft)

Photos: Tricia Ribble

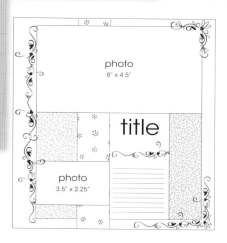

Supplies: Cardstock (Bazzill); patterned paper (Chatterbox); rub-ons (BasicGrey, Daisy D's); crystals (Prima); adhesive (3M, Beacon); Bernhard Fashion Italic font (Microsoft)

eye spy

Note how the black pen stroke framing the right side of this page creates the look of a faux mat, uniting the entire page.

The striking contrast of black does not make this layout any less feminine. In fact, combined with subtle shades of pink, blue and brown, the result is sophisticated and contemporary. An oversized title, repositioned to the left side of the page, entices the reader to discover the answer to such a bold statement. Candid journaling is offered in reply. Sparkling crystals intermingle between the title and patterned paper, fortifying the elegant design of the sketch.

The uncomplicated block structure of this sketch inspired Marla to "keep things simple" and keep the focus on her photos. The bold title integrates with her journaling, creating one unified element. Paper circles strung on a thin strip of paper trade places with the swirly design found on the sketch. A round sticker deftly positioned among the row of circles further chronicles the story the journaling imparts. Marla is indeed one of the coolest nerds I know, so the apple doesn't fall far from the tree!

Supplies: Cardstock (Bazzill); patterned paper (K&Co.); circle sticker (7gypsies); chipboard letters (BasicGrey, Pressed Petals); letter stickers (BasicGrey); stamp (Gel-à-tins); ink (Ranger); colored pencil; adhesive (3M); Jayne's Print font (Internet download)

Artwork: Marla Kress

Sketches translate well onto non-paper surfaces, as Judi proves with this eye-catching altered canvas. First, she tied two 6" x 12" (15cm x 30cm) canvases together with twine and then painted the edges with coordinating colors. After rotating the sketch counterclockwise, the rest of the elements fell into place. Judi replaced the feminine swirls depicted on the sketch with word stickers to reinforce the masculine design.

Supplies: Canvas (Dick Blick); patterned paper, word stickers (K&Co.); calendar stamp (Purple Onion); ink (StazOn); paint (Ranger); quote card (Fancy Pants); brad, photo turn (Jo-Ann's); adhesive (Golden, Therm O Web); hand drill (Fiskars)

Artwork: Judi VanValkinburgh

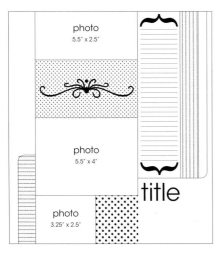

photo
5.5" x 2.5"

photo
5.5" x 4"

title

photo
3.25" x 2.5"

Mindy tailored this sketch to better suit her graphic style and the results make for an impressive, solid page. She first combined the two bottom photos into one focal photo, creating a visual column along the left side. The eye naturally wanders to the right, where it is met with clean, uninhibited journaling, ending in a candid, single-word title. Rounded page corners and a silk flower embellishment soften the look.

Supplies: Cardstock (KI Memories, Tinkering Ink); patterned paper (K&Co., Making Memories, Upsy Daisy); acetate word, chipboard, flower (Heidi Swapp); rub-on (K&Co.); adhesive (Tombow); Arial font (Microsoft)

Artwork: Mindy Bush

I never knew
that being a mom
could bring me
this much love,
joy, and pure
happiness! You
all make me so
grateful for each
and every day.
I'm thankful
for the blessings
you are in my life!
I always knew I
would love my
children, but I
never knew it
would be this
much!
Love, Mom

mine
joy

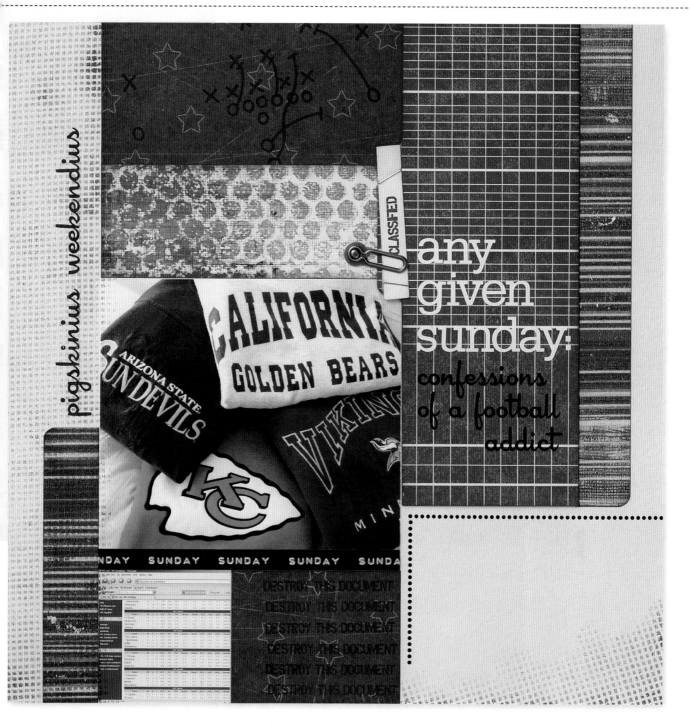

pigskinius weekendius

any given sunday: confessions of a football addict

CLASSIFIED

ARIZONA STATE SUN DEVILS

CALIFORNIA GOLDEN BEARS

VIKINGS

MINI

SUNDAY SUNDAY SUNDAY SUNDAY SUNDA

DESTROY THIS DOCUMENT
DESTROY THIS DOCUMENT
DESTROY THIS DOCUMENT
DESTROY THIS DOCUMENT
DESTROY THIS DOCUMENT
DESTROY THIS DOCUMENT

I admit it—my love of football borders on the obscene. In fact, unless you are on fire or dying, don't call me on a Sunday during football season. My full confession of this addiction is tucked behind a file folder marked "classified," securely closed with a photo turn. A hand-drawn quarterback sneak play takes the place of the top photo and the smaller photo at the bottom is a screenshot of the NFL standings, courtesy of www.nfl.com. Read fast—this page will self-destruct in thirty seconds.

Supplies: Cardstock (Bazzill); patterned paper (Adornit, Daisy D's, Dream Street, Mustard Moon); letter stickers, rub-on letters (American Crafts); dot rub-ons (One Heart); photo turn (7gypsies); brad, mesh (Making Memories); acrylic paint (Delta); stamps (Art Declassified); inks (Clearsnap, Ranger); adhesive (3M); pen (Sharpie); label (Dymo); Lucida Sans Unicode (Microsoft)

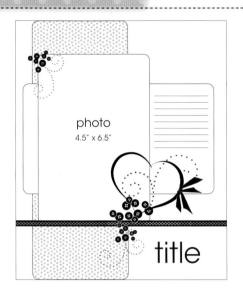

If you're a tried-and-true 12" x 12" (30cm x 30cm) scrapper, don't be quick to overlook other sketch sizes. Denine's layout proves how easy it is to convert an 8½" x 11" (22cm x 28cm) sketch to her preferred 12" x 12" (30cm x 30cm) format. She executed this layout beautifully on the roomier canvas, staying loyal to the substance of the sketch. Delightful details, such as hand stitching, strip journaling and a handcut title, yield a glimpse of Denine's true style: simple with a lot of TLC.

Supplies: Cardstock (Bazzill); patterned paper (BasicGrey); felt flowers (American Crafts); epoxy sticker (K&Co.); buttons, floss (Making Memories); ink (Clearsnap); corner rounder; adhesive (Glue Dots, Henkel); Century Gothic font (Microsoft)

Artwork: Denine Zielinski

tip: Instead of matting your photo on a separate piece of cardstock or paper, use the halo of white beyond the edges of your home-printed photo to create a matted look.

Simply put, Darby is a snow magnet. If there is a pile of the white stuff to be found, she's all over it. On this particular day, Chris had just shoveled the driveway, creating a nice, fluffy snow bank on the edge of the garage. Darby dove into one end of the pile and tunneled her way through, popping out on the other side. She had a look on her face as if to say, "Yeah, I'm cool!"

OK, all together now: "Awwwww, look at the puppy!" Yep, she's a cutie all right. With a toothbrush and a bit of watered-down white paint, I spattered the chipboard letters of the title and the plastic snowflakes to create a faux snow effect. One of the snowflakes takes the place of the "O" in my title and a double layer of smaller snowflakes attached to the top left corner adds balance, keeping the focus on my photo. The contrast of the dark background paper makes all the elements pop off the page. Although the sketch illustrates a heart embellishment, other shapes (such as the snowflakes here) will drive the theme of your page.

Supplies: Cardstock (Bazzill); patterned paper (Bo-Bunny, My Mind's Eye); snowflakes (Heidi Swapp); chipboard letters (Imagination Project); letter stickers (BasicGrey); large snaps (We R Memory Keepers); acrylic paint (Delta); sandpaper; toothbrush; adhesive (3M, Glue Dots); ITC American Typewriter font (Microsoft)

3.

Nothing is more thoughtful than to send someone a homemade card. With a bit of imagination and creative thinking on a smaller scale, many sketches easily convert to cards, particularly the 8½" x 11" (22cm x 28cm) format. Shawna took one sketch and translated it into three terrific cards.

1. **Yo card supplies:** Cardstock (Bazzill); patterned paper (Daisy D's); fabric flowers (We R Memory Keepers); paper flowers (Prima); letters (Daisy D's, Scrap Essentials); adhesive (3M, Sakura); buttons

2. **Hugs & kisses card supplies:** Cardstock (Bazzill); patterned paper (Urban Lily); stamps (Li'l Davis); ink (Stampin' Up); paper flowers (Prima); adhesive (3M); brads; silk flowers

3. **Peace card supplies:** Cardstock (Bazzill); patterned paper (Arctic Frog); fabric (Weavewerks); brads, embossing powder, picture hanger, stamps (Stampin' Up); ink (VersaMark); adhesive (3M); silk flower

Artwork: Shawna Martinez, *Friend of PageMaps*

2.

1.

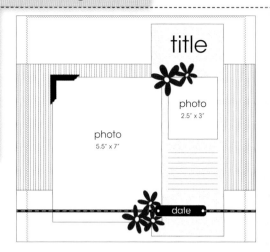

title

photo
2.5" x 3"

photo
5.5" x 7"

date

What do you get when you combine one very cute kid, an assortment of vibrant papers and a few dazzling embellishments? A very colorful layout filled with energy and oomph! Notwithstanding all the eye candy on this page, the most creative part is the quilt fabric binding that frames the entire layout and takes the stitches illustrated on the sketch over the top. Now that's cool!

Supplies: Cardstock (Bazzill, Die Cuts With A View); patterned paper (BasicGrey, Scenic Route, Stemma); border sticker (My Mind's Eye); chipboard (Junkitz); transparency (Hambly); fabric strips (Weavewerks); silk flower

Artwork: Becky Heisler, *Friend of PageMaps*

A clever play off the title of this page provides a repetitive word that appears throughout a field of thought-provoking quotes and takes the place of the second photo on the sketch. A large hand-cut bracket emphasizes the entire title, while a smaller bracket pulls out the word "IF," accentuated in a contrasting color. A large photo of an oak tree, thought by many to be the tree of life, plays a supporting role on the layout.

Supplies: Cardstock (Bazzill); patterned paper (Chatterbox); metal letters (American Crafts); flower stamp (Gel-à-tins); ink (VersaMark); eyelets (Doodlebug); decorative scissors; circle punches; adhesives (3M, Glue Dots); Arriere Guarde, Stack fonts (Internet downloads)

Yo, yo, yo. Whazzup up with this layout, huh? Dude, it's got some bling bling goin' on. Word. You'll pardon my street speak, but this layout was the bomb diggity to create! Playing off the bold, vivid colors found in the pattern paper truly drove the rest of the design for this page. With this poppin' patterned paper, I can honestly say, "There ain't much else you gotta do to da page, dawg." When working with chaotic or wild patterns, a good rule to follow is, "less is more." That's when a simple sketch like this one is a perfect choice.

Supplies: Cardstock (Bazzill); patterned paper (Rouge de Garance); rhinestones; (Heidi Swapp, L'Orna, Making Memories); pearl brad, velvet flower (Imaginisce); acrylic letters (KI Memories); velvet symbol (Making Memories); resin sticker (Stemma); adhesives (3M, Glue Dots); Carbonated Gothic font (Internet download)

Photos: Tricia Ribble

tip: When I first completed this layout, the lime green strip of paper really popped off the page, competing with my homies' photos. Matting the entire layout on the same green paper brought that wicked-cool color under control.

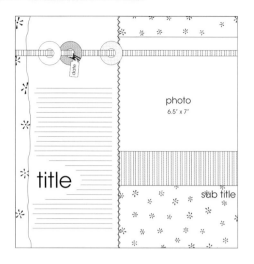

When I filled up the journaling area on this sketch with the multiple-choice questions, I realized I had no space left to explain the silly exam. Necessity being the mother of invention, I looked at my photo (which, clearly, my husband took given the fact that part of my head is cut off) and discovered a nifty, dark spot to tuck my journaling in. The washers on the sketch were traded for male and female symbols (boy, tell me those aren't anatomically correct!) that I covered with crackle medium. Rhinestones serve as answers to the tomboy questions, resulting in an oxymoronic embellishment for the page. Hey, I might not sparkle too often, but my page sure does!

Supplies: Patterned paper, velvet ribbon (BasicGrey); letter stickers (American Crafts); crackle medium (Ranger); rhinestones (Heidi Swapp); male and female chipboard symbols (artist's design); chalk (Stampin' Up); thread; adhesive (3M, Tombow); Another Typewriter font (Microsoft)

tip: Rubbing black chalk into the cracks of the iconic symbols really accented the glass-like fractures.

Whoa, dude—now that's a blue tongue! Strong, saturated photos like these require little in the way of attention-grabbing paper. After flipping the sketch horizontally, I used horizontally striped patterned paper that naturally leads the eye across the page. After printing the journaling on a swatch of white cardstock, I created a faux embossed texture by adhering die-cut swirls in the same white cardstock. A subtitle bisects the journaling, reinforcing the theme of this silly page.

Supplies: Cardstock (Bazzill); letter stickers, patterned paper (Arctic Frog); brads, photo turns (Queen & Co.); die-cut swirl (Sizzix); epoxy letters (KI Memories); rick-rack (Doodlebug); ink (Ranger); circle cutter; die-cut tags (Provo Craft); adhesive (3M, Glue Dots); Avant Garde font (Microsoft)

Photos: Tricia Ribble

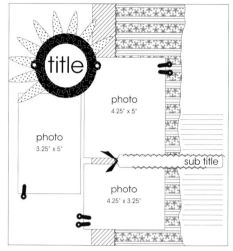

---

tip: For added dimension, double up photo anchors one on top of the other and attach with a brad.

Staying true to her wonderful, linear style, Mindy first squared up all the elements on this sketch to an even, horizontal position. Doing so allowed room for a larger focal photo of her darling daughter Saige. An uninterrupted piece of apple green scalloped cardstock bridges the entire span of the top third of the page, where a bold title rests above it. Eye-catching color harmony unifies the rest of this simple, yet stylish, page and the rub-ons add a touch of whimsy. That is one cool hat!

Supplies: Scalloped cardstock (Bazzill); patterned paper, rub-ons (K&Co.); ribbon (Making Memories); adhesive (Tombow); Garamond font (Microsoft); Tommy Hilfiger font (Internet download)

Artwork: Mindy Bush

'CHASE'·ING FALL

By November, it had already snowed and Colorado's early winter had pretty much chased autumn away, but we still managed to pile up a few leaves for some fun. Playing in the fallen leaves is one of Chase's favorite fall activities. This year was no exception and, even though there weren't very many leaves left, we made the best of it and Chase had a lot of fun!

Chase 11-16-06

No, that's not a typo! A twist on Chase's name segued into an amusing play on words for this page's title. As illustrated on the sketch, I created a four-piece frame from paper-covered chipboard, then tied them together with embroidery floss where the pieces intersect. The chipboard leaf embellishment that graces the top of the frame strengthened the fall theme, and sanding the edges of the earth-toned papers added a weathered texture similar to the dry, autumn leaves in the photos.

Supplies: Cardstock (Bazzill); patterned paper (A2Z, Fancy Pants, Fontwerks, Imaginisce); chipboard letters (Chatterbox); chipboard leaves (CherryArte); chipboard label, Precision File Set (BasicGrey); chipboard, metal tab (Making Memories); adhesive (3M, GlueDots); floss (DMC); decorative scissors; Cipher font (Internet download)

Photos: Tricia Ribble

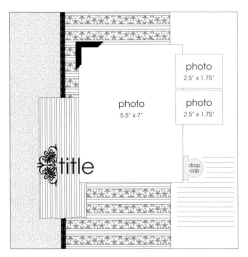

I've often wondered what profession I would have chosen had I arrived on this earth one hundred years earlier. After donning this attire for a portrait, I can confidently say I would not have been a dance hall girl strutting about the saloons! This page reads like an old western "WANTED" poster, riddled with bullet holes, burned edges and western-style fonts to add authenticity to the theme. I replaced the two small photos from the sketch in the upper right corner with open white space to lend a bit of "breathing" room (since there wasn't any in the corset!). You know, I think I would have made a great Annie Oakley.

Supplies: Cardstock (Bazzill); patterned paper (Dream Street, Flair, K&Co., Melissa Frances); ink (7gypsies, Ranger); die-cut shape (Autumn Leaves); chipboard scroll (Cactus Pink); bar pin (K&Co.); metal brads (Making Memories); rub-ons (My Mind's Eye); adhesives (3M, Glue Dots); poker chip; Adobe Wood Cuts, Euphorigenic fonts (Internet downloads)

eye spy

An authentic poker chip, aged with a bit of ink, becomes a date holder and a lead-in to the journaling.

This "charming" layout is another great example of how you can convert sketches from one size to another. Judi adapted the original 12" x 12" (30cm x 30cm) sketch to her favorite 8½" x 11" (22cm x 28cm) format, yet maintained continuity in the organization of the page. The serendipitous photo of her adorable daughter Charlotte was the inspiration for this layout. Spunky chipboard stars take the place of the two smaller photos, and instead of a block of journaling, handwritten notes are inscribed on overlapping circles. The coup de grâce of this gorgeous layout is the right edge of the page where Judi trimmed a playful, scalloped curve. What a charming idea!

Supplies: Cardstock (Bazzill); cardstock stickers, chipboard shapes, patterned paper (Heidi Grace); chipboard letters (My Little Shoebox); brads (American Crafts); decorative tape, photo corner (Heidi Swapp); dimensional glitter (Ranger); ribbon (Maya Road); decorative scissors; adhesive (Henkel, Therm O Web, Tombow)

Artwork: Judi VanValkinburgh

On this layout, I wanted to use a bold title for a big statement so I added brackets around the number eight to create a play on words to the well-known catchphrase, "high five." To house such a large title, I rotated the sketch clockwise. The celebration theme carries throughout the page with hand-made, chipboard candles capped with stars. Falling stars cling to vertical lines of stitching, communicating a subliminal "Make a Wish" message.

Supplies: Patterned paper, letter stickers (American Crafts); chipboard brackets (BasicGrey); rub-ons (Daisy D's); thread; adhesive (3M, Zig); American Typewriter font (Microsoft)

It's hard to imagine that more than sixty million buffalo once roamed North America, but they are alive and well in Yellowstone National Park. This layout pays homage to this venerable beast, complete with a meandering trail of hand-drawn hoofprints that walk right off the page. A western-style print joins contemporary stripes for a unique mixture of color and dimension. A continuous single sewing stitch frames the photos and journaling, and additional sewing details border the edges of the focal photo as illustrated on the sketch.

Supplies: Cardstock (Bazzill); patterned paper (Crate Paper, My Mind's Eye, Pebbles); rub-ons (Fancy Pants); adhesive (3M); thread; buffalo tracks (artist's own design); Combustion Wide BRK, Oklahoma font (Internet downloads)

eye (spy)

The use of a western-style font in the title and subtitle reinforces the "way out west" appeal of this page.

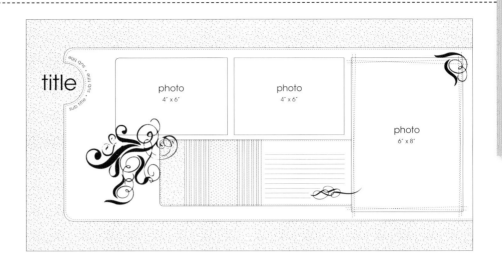

Bathed in a watery palette of azure blue and sea green, there's no mistaking the beach theme of this layout. A quick horizontal flip of the sketch moved the focal photo to the left, featuring a family photo framed in wavy swirls. Smaller, supporting photos stream off to the right, where they converge with an impressive, hand-cut corner embellishment. A Spanish title adds authenticity to this Cancun-inspired page.

Supplies: Cardstock (Bazzill); patterned paper (Autumn Leaves, My Mind's Eye, One Heart One Mind, Rouge de Garance); chipboard letters (K&Co.); die-cut flowers (Rouge de Garance); glass beads (Mill Hill); glitter (Melissa Frances); rub-ons (Martha Stewart); digital brush by Rhonna Farrer (Two Peas in a Bucket); adhesive (3M); Goudy Old Style font (Microsoft)

Photos: Tricia Ribble

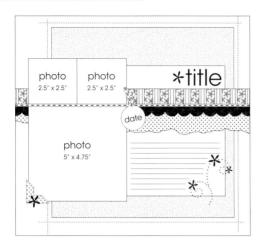

A set of nine wooden blocks and Marla's incredible imagination produced this amazing altered puzzle set. When assembled, each of the six sides displays a full mini layout based on the sketch. What a great piece of artwork! A simple sketch with minimal details works best for a project like this. Read on for tips on how you can make a wooden block project of your own.

Supplies: Wooden blocks (Creative Imaginations); cardstock (Bazzill); letter stickers, patterned paper (BasicGrey); adhesive (3M); Dear Joe font (Internet download)

Artwork: Marla Kress

tips:

- When creating the layouts, keep layers to a minimum; otherwise the blocks will not fit tightly together.

- Apply clear contact paper to the top of each layout for added protection before cutting them into squares.

- Use a straightedge and a sharp craft knife to cut the layouts apart; paper trimmers tend to pull while cutting and the squares will not be uniform.

- Avoid bulky embellishments. Use patterned paper to find your embellishments, isolating images that go with your page theme.

- Instead of stitching, use colored pencils, pens, markers or rub-ons to create a border.

- When designing each page, take note of cut lines and place your photos accordingly to avoid cutting off a person's head.

- Spray adhesive works great for applying the cut squares to the wooden blocks.

Customized labels are a breeze with a label maker. Carefully remove the label tape from your label maker.

Trim a piece of heavy paper or cardstock the same width as the label tape (most are just shy of ⅜" wide) and feed the piece, pattern side up, into the back of the label maker.

Advance the strip the desired length, then squeeze out your message on the dial.

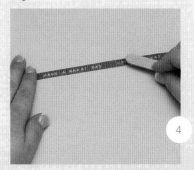

Lightly sand or ink the tops of the embossed letters to help them stand out.

The linear simplicity of this sketch belies the many small details found on the layout, starting with a title that briefly gives one pause. Oversized, corrugated letters stand out and say "Hey!" with the help of a swipe of white paint across the top ridges. My label maker did doubleduty, not only serving as part of the title, but also creating the coffee banner bisecting the two photos. Swirly rub-ons applied to a colorful close-up of my coffee mug create a faux steam meandering out of the creamy foam. Finally, the bottom of a coffee mug dipped in watered-down ink and set down directly on the page replicates the coffee ring frequently found on my desk blotter. Like stamping, this particular technique is not one I would recommend if you've just had caffeine!

Supplies: Cardstock (Bazzill, WorldWin); patterned paper (Dream Street, Flair); Kraft letters (Rusty Pickle); rub-on (BasicGrey); ink (Ranger); chalk (Pebbles); acrylic paint (Delta); label (Dymo); thread; adhesive (3M, Glue Dots); Gauntlet Classic font (Internet download)

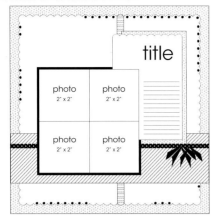

Whimsical, glittery angel wings attached to Kylie's back add an amusing, angelic touch to this layout.

There's no harm in breaking a creative tenet, especially when your photos command it. With sequential photos such as these, I decided to convert the four-square photo block into a circle, which instantly added motion to the page. One clockwise rotation of the sketch and the rest of the design fell into place. Fuzzy letter stickers and glittery snowflakes falling down the page capture the essence of the wintry, frosty theme, all in an unexpected color combination of bright pinks and lime greens (and a bit of shimmery blue for good measure).

Supplies: Cardstock (Bazzill); patterned paper (Imagination Project); letter stickers (Making Memories); glitter angel wings (Melissa Frances); glitter snowflake buttons (Dress It Up); adhesive (3M, Glue Dots); Romantha font (Internet download)

Photos: Tricia Ribble

Lita's first visit to the ocean produced a huge grin and the first words out of her mouth were, "This is big!" Tiffany slightly adapted the photo collage from the sketch to include three photos instead of four and moved the title of the page to the bottom left corner to ground the layout. Maintaining focus on the delightful photos of her daughter, the layers were built up using soft, contrasting colors. Tiffany's narrative journaling wraps around the right side of the photo collage, drawing the eye to the center of the page.

Supplies: Cardstock (WorldWin); patterned paper (Bo-Bunny, K&Co., Making Memories); chipboard letters (Making Memories); brads, chipboard stickers (Cloud 9); tags (Avery); photo frame sticker (Sandylion); adhesive (3L); Georgia font (Microsoft)

Artwork: Tiffany Tillman

This moment has been a long time coming ... your first encounter with the beach. It's almost like a mini-right of passage to me because I have lived near a beach all my life. Actually, land locked isn't really a part of my vocabulary. When we moved to Dallas, I knew I would miss the seafood but what I really missed was the smell of the salt in the ocean and that ocean breeze. You can't experience that when you're land locked and small lakes don't even compare. I was relieved when your Dad and I decided we could finally return back to 'home'. And I think my heart was giddy coming back to the place which I too first saw at the age of three/four: The Beach. I will never forget this though. On seeing the ocean for the first time, you stretched your arms as wide as you could and said, "This is big!" I think we were on the same page.

ocean

big

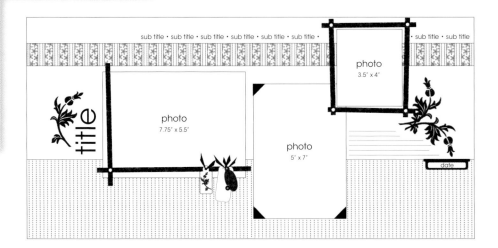

Like any young boy, Chase is enthusiastic about any outdoor activity. His Super Flyer kite took flight on the first try, and these photos captured his intense focus as he kept his new toy airborne. The stitched rub-ons that extend as tails of the kite add motion and energy to the spread while drawing the eye to the focal point, which is further highlighted with a circle of brads. Simple journaling in the form of a quote from the photo subject adds flavor and authenticity. A large kite, made of vellum and chipboard, houses the book-style title.

Supplies: Cardstock (Bazzill); patterned paper (Pebbles, Scenic Route); vellum (Prism); letter stickers (BasicGrey); rub-ons (Creative Imaginations, Die Cuts With A View); snaps (Doodlebug, We R Memory Keepers); grommets (Making Memories); adhesive (3M, Glue Dots); chipboard; ribbon; Tork font (Internet download)

Photos: Tricia Ribble

I admit it: I'm an uncomformist. If you tell me how something should be done, there's a very good possibility that I'll do it another way. As you can see, the sketch on this page is meant to be a double layout. But as I studied it, I really liked the left side of the sketch and saw the potential for a single layout. So, true to my nature, that's exactly what I did. With a bit of creative adjustment and rotation, a nice design came together. Playing off the large polka dots in the patterned paper, I intertwined my journaling around the printed elements. For added dimension, I ran my thumbnail over the petals of the die-cut flowers, curling them upward. My creative mantra? When in doubt, change it.

Supplies: Cardstock (Bazzill); die-cuts, patterned paper (Wübe); letter stickers (American Crafts); chipboard tags (BasicGrey); sheer ribbon (Offray); chipboard; thread; decorative scissors; brads (Making Memories); adhesive (3M, Glue Dots); Nilland font (Internet download)

Photo: Amy Goldstein

tip: After converting your photo to black and white, does it look too bold and harsh? Try the "Diffuse Glow" filter in your favorite image-editing program to soften and tone down your image.

one sketch, three ways

3

The Merriam-Webster dictionary defines the word style as, "a particular manner or technique by which something is done, created or performed." Without a doubt, scrapbook pages are as individual as the artists who create them. Several talented friends join me in this chapter to interpret ten sketches, each of us applying our own unique and personal touches and experimenting with various techniques and trends. With such diverse and distinct creative spirits, there are sure to be pages that resonate with your individual style.

As the pages of this chapter came together, I was constantly amazed at each artist's take on a sketch and had many, "Why didn't I think of that?" moments. I hope you will, too.

> Creativity requires the courage to let go of certainties. **Erich Fromm**

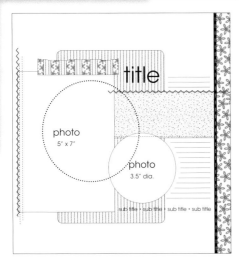

Supplies: Cardstock (Bazzill); patterned paper (K&Co., Heidi Grace); die-cut border (Scribble Scrabble); brad, flower (Heidi Swapp); rub-ons, stickers (K&Co.); lace (Fancy Pants); letter stickers (American Crafts); journaling sticker (Creative Imaginations); vintage Holly Hobby cupcake pick (Ebay); adhesive (Henkel, Therm O Web, Tombow)

Artwork: Judi VanValkinburgh

tip: Don't feel that you have to match colors perfectly on a layout. Mixing patterns and colors in different tones and hues adds interest. A light or white background will draw all your elements together.

When Judi was a little girl, one of her birthday cakes had a similar decoration as the Holly Hobby cake pick that topped the cupcakes at her twin daughters' third birthday party. This memory is cleverly intertwined in her modern, yet vintage, page by using one of the cake picks as an embellishment. After a quick horizontal reverse of the sketch, Judi brought together various shades of pink and green papers to strengthen the girly charm of the page. A delightful pink title that follows the curve of the flower adds a playful touch. This layout is so sweet!

This sketch employs the rule of thirds with an interesting twist: The title bisects the journaling. This is a great solution to a journaling-intensive page because it breaks up the text into smaller, more readable portions. After printing the title on white cardstock, it felt rather bland. My solution? I chose four acrylic paint colors found in the striped paper and, with an old toothbrush, spattered the colors across a piece of white cardstock. Once dry, I reprinted my title. I used a large, but unobtrusive, rub-on in place of the sewing details found on the left side of the sketch. A repeat of the striped paper at the top and bottom of the photos brings focus to the subject and a swirly tendril of painted dots identifies the source of the close-up photo.

Supplies: Cardstock (Bazzill); patterned paper (Bo-Bunny, Daisy Bucket, Sweetwater); chipboard scroll (Fancy Pants); rub-on (Daisy D's); acrylic paint (Junkitz); thread; adhesive (3M); ITC American Typewriter font (Internet download)

You bought me a sweet and simple gift just the other day. It was a John Legend CD and I'm sad to admit it was my first time really hearing his music. He is, by far, fantastic.
us
One song called Ordinary People plays on that CD which brought me to tears the first time I heard it. I think, I know, it's the first song I have ever heard which clearly explains everything we've been through and put it each other through. And in the car on a regular Sunday drive, I played the song for you and you knew it too.
We've made our mistakes in our relationship; we are equally responsible. We've told our lies, shared our wisdoms, and loved each other throughout. We've screamed, we've cried, and sometimes – maybe once or twice – we've taken our anger too far. But right now, this evening, we still love each other and still stick it through. After all, we are just ordinary people.
INARY PEOPLE • ORDINARY PEOPLE • ORDINARY PEOPLE • ORDINARY

Tiffany's page title was inspired by the song "Ordinary People" by John Legend and her tender, candid journaling reflects that, despite a few bumps in the road, she and her husband are indeed just ordinary people. To maintain a strong focus on her photos and words, this page needed very little in the way of embellishments. Circular photos, wrapped text and complementary patterned paper complete this well-executed layout.

Supplies: Cardstock (WorldWin); patterned paper (Chatterbox); letter stickers (Making Memories); adhesive (3L); Georgia font (Microsoft)

Artwork: Tiffany Tillman

give it a try

Follow these simple instructions for wrapping text around a circle using Microsoft Word.

1. First, trim two photos into a circle; one should be larger than the other. Measure the diameter of the smaller circle. Set aside.

2. Open a new document in Microsoft Word. Type the journaling. Adjust the margins of the text to fit on the scrapbook page.

3. Go to Insert > Picture > Auto Shape. Select Basic Shapes from the tool bar and then select the Oval Shape. Hold down the shift key and click and drag the mouse to draw a circle.

4. Double click the new circle; the Format Auto Shape menu will open. Select the Layout tab and set the wrapping style to Tight and the Alignment to Other. Now select the Size tab and enter the dimension of the measured circle photo. An additional quarter inch (6mm) or half inch (13mm) may be added to the final dimension to add space between the journaling text and photo. With the menu still open, select the Color and Line tab. Change the fill color to No Fill and the line color to No Line. Click OK.

5. Use the mouse to select the circle and position your circle intersecting the journaling. The journaling should tightly wrap around the hidden circle leaving a space to attach a photo. Print the page on cardstock and adhere the photo into the knocked-out space.

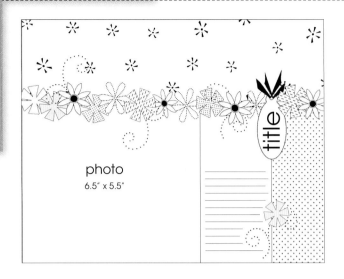

photo
6.5" x 5.5"

title

Clearly (no pun intended!), I ditched the band of flowers depicted on the sketch and replaced them with a horizontal strip of transparency. I attached an assortment of white rub-ons to the back of the clear plastic for some added oomph. Like a footnote in a book, the oversized asterisk next to the title draws the reader to the journaling in search of the fine print. To keep the elements from competing with one another, this page maintains a strong, graphic design.

Supplies: Cardstock, brads (Bazzill); chipboard elements, patterned paper (Cosmo Cricket); transparency (Hammermill); chipboard letters (Li'l Davis); texture plate (Fiskars); die-cut flower (Provo Craft); chipboard tag, rub-ons (BasicGrey); adhesive (3M, Therm O Web); Marydale font (Internet download)

* You and me, we go together nicely. We're like peanut butter and jelly. Where it gets tricky is deciding on white bread or whole wheat. You are a "plan it out" kind of guy and I like to fly by the seat of my pants. You need a date and time and I'm spontaneous. You're quiet and reserved and I have a big mouth and talk too much. You are serious and I'm a comedian. But where the bread doesn't matter is when it comes to the things we love. We dig fly fishing. We both love to camp. Our hearts race at the mere mention of football. We adore our furry family. We trust one another. Our friendship is strong. We've learned to switch between white and whole wheat. Yep, we make a good pair, you and me.

Rather than rotating the entire sketch vertically, Mindy employed a better solution for her tall photo: she rotated all the elements within the sketch vertically. The result is this stunningly simple, yet elegant, page about her benevolent daughters, Saige and Ally. A computer-generated title is modestly superimposed over the photo, and the same font is echoed in reverse type in her journaling block, discreetly hugged in white, scalloped edges. A loose-hanging floral tag adds to the casual feel of the page.

Supplies: Patterned paper (Making Memories, Tinkering Ink); felt embellishment (Tinkering Ink); tag (Avery); chipboard flowers (Making Memories); adhesive (Glue Dots, Therm O Web); Chanl font (Internet download)

Artwork: Mindy Bush

Something that stands out immediately on this eye-catching page is the absence of one solid piece of patterned paper across the top, as the sketch depicts. In its place, Patti attached six various widths of coordinating paper strips, sewn in place in a quilt-like fashion. Machine stitching details continue throughout the layout, adding to the vintage, yet contemporary, feel of the page. To create her flower embellishments, Patti punched out circles from patterned paper, and then cut five wedges out of each circle, forming the petals. Single adjectives, in piece journaling fashion, describe her beautiful, young daughter Sheridan.

Supplies: Cardstock (Prism); patterned paper (Adornit, Bo-Bunny, Mustard Moon); die-cut punches (Fiskars, Marvy); ink (Clearsnap); lace (Fancy Pants); brads (Making Memories); dimensional paint (Ranger); adhesive (Xyron); Berlin font (Internet download)

Artwork: Patti Milazzo, *Friend of PageMaps*

eye spy

Did you notice the dimensional dots of pearl paint inside several of the paper flowers?

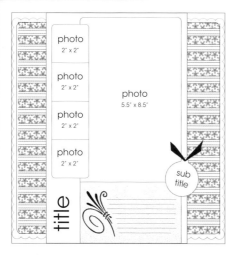

This sketch, with a strip of four small photos, presented the perfect opportunity for Marla to scrap ultrasound photos of her yet-to-be-born daughter, Adeline. These petite snapshots are amazing, and the precious focal photo bears witness to her final arrival. Tender journaling meanders around a precision-cut vine, where dimensional flower stickers are randomly scattered. The entire layout, turned counterclockwise, rests on a bold piece of black cardstock, unified by the black photo matting and circular-framed title.

Supplies: Cardstock (Bazzill); patterned paper (Making Memories); flower stickers (K&Co.); chipboard frame (Imagination Project); label stickers (7gypsies); chipboard letters (Heidi Swapp); vine pattern (artist's own design); adhesive (3M); Georgia font (Microsoft); LHF Sophia Script font (Internet download)

Artwork: Marla Kress

Team spirit abounds on this layout about my husband's alma mater playing in the 2004 Holiday Bowl. It is no stretch to say that Chris is obsessed with the Cal Bears and our joint logo-driven wardrobes are a dead giveaway. A selection of three long-distance field shots, matted in white, take the place of the four smaller photos found on the sketch. A selection of patterned and solid papers supports the team colors, and the alumni button and ticket stubs "bear" proof that we were at the big game. Go Bears!

Supplies: Cardstock (Bazzill); patterned paper (Scenic Route); fabric label (Me & My Big Ideas); chipboard letters (KI Memories); acrylic paint (Delta); adhesive (3M); Arriere Garde font (Internet download); game mementos

The playful spirit of this page is cheered on with a palette of crayon colors and photos of one cute kid. Denine broke up the strip of mini photos found on the sketch and stacked them irregularly, one on top of another, each embellished with a button and tiny tag defining Ryan's steps on how to drink hot cocoa. Another set of buttons frolics at the bottom right corner, and the sweet journaling buoys the lighthearted theme of this page.

Supplies: Cardstock (Die Cuts With A View); patterned paper (American Crafts); chipboard heart (Fancy Pants); chipboard accent (Urban Lily); buttons (American Crafts, Making Memories); brads (Making Memories); jewelry tags (Avery); die-cut punches; adhesive (EK Success, Glue Dots); Avant Garde font (Internet download); Century Gothic font (Microsoft)

Artwork: Denine Zielinski

eye spy

Fastening buttons with colorful mini brads added another tactile dimension to this page.

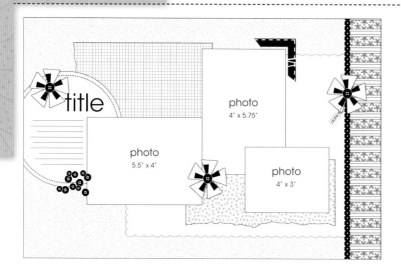

On this page I replaced the flowers and buttons on the sketch with paw prints and pebbles to reflect the theme. I really dig clear embellishments, but often they do not show up well on a page. To give my title added oomph, I painted the backs of the acrylic letters with coordinating green craft paint. The journaling begins below the title in somewhat of a fairy-tale jargon, and then abruptly ends with three ellipses. With a borrowed line from famous radio personality Paul Harvey, the reader is enticed to lift the magnetic closure, attached to the left photo, to learn "the rest of the story."

Supplies: Cardstock (Prism); patterned paper (My Mind's Eye, Paper Loft, Sweetwater, We R Memory Keepers); magnetic tieback (BasicGrey); canvas frame (Li'l Davis); twill (Shoebox Trims); ribbon (May Arts, Scenic Route); ink (Ranger); die-cut tag (Provo Craft); acrylic letters (Go West); stamps (Adornit); circle cutter (EK Success); acrylic paint (Delta); pebbles; adhesive (3M, Aleene's, KI Memories, Tombow); Avant Garde font (Microsoft)

Judi has lived in or near Niagara Falls for more than thirty years, but until a friend's visit to the area, she had never experienced one of its oldest and most popular attractions: a ride on the Maid of the Mist. The name of the boat inspired her clever, play-on-words title, which she chose to feature big and bold instead of enclosed within the circle as portrayed on the sketch. Decorative chipboard, painted a beautiful aqua and dotted in pearl white dimensional paint, serves as splashes of water on this nautical-themed layout.

Supplies: Cardstock (Bazzill, Prism); patterned paper (Bo-Bunny, K&Co.); coaster accents (Imagination Project); brads (SEI); chipboard (Maya Road); ribbon (American Crafts); acrylic paint, liquid pearls (Ranger); stickers (7gypsies); decorative punch (Marvy); decorative scissors; adhesive (Henkel, Therm O Web, Tombow)'

Artwork: Judi VanValkinburgh

Rich in a palette of youthful, primary colors, the papers Sheredian chose for her layout mimic the artistic endeavors of her sweet grandson Christian. Star embellishments are scattered about the page, taking the place of the flowers illustrated on the sketch. Single word accolades serve as journaling between two stamped brackets. This layout gets a gold star!

Supplies: Patterned paper (Paper Loft); brads, letter stickers (American Crafts): stamps (Autumn Leaves); ink (Clearsnap, Stampin' Up); chipboard heart, star (Heidi Swapp); corner punch; chipboard letter (EK Success); brads, chipboard star, ribbon (Making Memories); buttons (Dress It Up); adhesive (3M, Fabric Tack, Glue Dots, Tombow)

Artwork: Sheredian Vickers, *Friend of PageMaps*

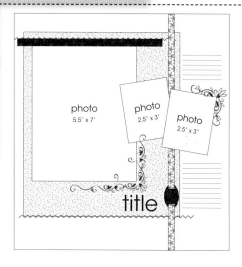

photo
5.5˝ x 7˝

photo
2.5˝ x 3˝

photo
2.5˝ x 3˝

title

Tiffany flipped the sketch horizontally and split the large, single photo into two. Strip journaling, printed in reverse type, subdues the bright pink patterned paper, and tells the hilarious story of how poor Lita's little lips got so darn big. The conversational tone of the journaling adds to the humorous theme of the page. Chipboard photo corners lined up in a downward slant supply direction to the order of the photos.

Supplies: Cardstock (Prism); patterned paper (Scenic Route, SEI); chipboard heart and letters (Heidi Swapp); epoxy sticker (KI Memories); frame (Making Memories); photo corners (Scenic Route); ink (Ranger); adhesive (3L); Serifa BT font (Internet download)

Artwork: Tiffany Tillman

eye (spy)

Notice how Tiffany allowed a couple of her journaling strips to casually fall off the edge of the page. Don't be afraid to leave the confines of your background paper!

With black-and-white photos, the sky is the limit when it comes to paper and color choices. Here, Mindy stayed true to her classic, chic style and chose understated tones of green, brown and orange. A top and bottom row of stitched rub-ons brings focus to the main photo. To accommodate her high-contrast white title, she moved the two supporting photos toward the bottom, leaving just enough room for a one-word description of her son Brig.

Supplies: Cardstock (Bazzill); patterned paper (Upsy Daisy); chipboard title (Heidi Swapp); rub-ons (K&Co.); letter and number stickers (Making Memories); adhesive (Therm O Web); Garamond font (Microsoft)

Artwork: Mindy Bush

With a wild fire nipping at our property line and less than 10 minutes to heed the Sheriff's order to evacuate, to say the situation was intense is an understatement.

As I quickly hustled the cats and dogs into the truck, my mind was racing, trying to make mental notes of what else I should take. Boxes of photos and albums were obvious. I grabbed the laptop, camera, and external hard drive and shoved them into the back seat. I threw our daily meds and a change of clothes into an overnight bag, hitched up Chris's guiding boat, and pulled out of the driveway with just moments to spare.

Driving away from the ranch, watching in my rear view mirror as smoke billowed a thousand feet into the sky, I realized all that I had forgotten to take. My antique cookbooks, my grandma's Austrian crystal, my grandpa's wheat penny collection, Chris's mementos marking a 23-year career in the Marine Corps. So much that could be lost and never replaced.

Later that evening, Mother Nature blessed us with a shifting wind and pushed the fire away from the ranch. Although relieved, I had much empathy for neighbors and friends who lost homes, buildings, fences, pastures and hay.

We were allowed back on the ranch several days later but the scars of the Saunders Fire still remain today, reminding us of how close we came to losing everything.

fire on the mountain

This sketch is ideal for a layout with lengthy journaling, and because I had such an intense focal photo, I decided to flip the sketch horizontally, placing the large photo on the right. It is no secret that I am a maverick when it comes to scrapbooking, and I say this to qualify the "technique" I tried on this layout. I really wanted to drive home the idea of fire on this page, so I carefully burned a large hole through the photo and underlying pattern paper, creating an opening to house my title. Taking this idea one step further, I also singed the outer edges of the bandana patterned paper. Granted, all of this could have been achieved through tearing and inking, but I wanted to lend the page an air of authenticity. Black crystals, in a smoke and flame pattern, add a dramatic effect. (As with any technique using fire, take proper precautions for ventilation and safety.)

Supplies: Cardstock (Bazzill); patterned paper (7gypsies, Crate Paper, Flair); letter stickers (SEI); file set (BasicGrey); rhinestones (Prima); ink (Ranger); adhesive (3M); Baar Sophia font (Internet download)

When I came across this verse, I asked my friend Marla if I could use a sleeping photo of her infant daughter Adeline. I could not have asked for a more perfect, tranquil photo to complement this sonnet. Beaded chipboard scrolls replace the brackets found on the sketch and serve as anchors on the journaling panel. The font used for the hand-cut title resonates in the adjectives of the verse. Petite pearl beads are scattered about the top half of the page, adding to the serene quality of the layout.

Supplies: Cardstock (Paper Company); patterned paper (Heidi Grace); chipboard scrolls (Maya Road); plastic flowers (Heidi Grace); rub-ons (Déjà Views); glass beads (Mill Hill); micro beads (Darice); acrylic paint (Delta); dimensional adhesive (Plaid); adhesives (3M, Glue Dots); decorative scissors; thread; Bernhard Modern, LT Zapfino fonts (Internet downloads)

Photo: Marla Kress

1 Paint edges and surface of chipboard with a coordinating color (or contrasting color, depending on the look you'd like to achieve). Allow to dry.

2 Apply an even coat of clear dimensional glue to the chipboard.

3 While wet, sprinkle on a mixture of glass seed beads and press lightly with your finger.

4 Fill in any gaps with clear micro beads. Set aside to dry completely; shake off excess beads.

Single photo sketches afford a great opportunity to use bold, large print papers without risking the patterns overwhelming your subject, and Marla's layout is a great example. Armed with a terrific shot of her adorable son Liam, she balanced out the large floral pattern with an equally bold title, topped with a handmade felt cherry. Elongated journaling, framed inside brackets, and a vertically striped pattern spanning the bottom half of the page bring together the layers of the page.

Supplies: Cardstock (Bazzill); felt accent, patterned paper (Tinkering Ink); letter stickers (American Crafts, Making Memories); bookplate, brads (Making Memories); date stamp (Purple Onion); rub-ons (KI Memories); ink (Ranger); adhesive (3M); felt; Georgia, Impact fonts (Microsoft)

Artwork: Marla Kress

Nothing is more precious than a photo exemplifying the love of two siblings and in Mindy's relaxed, yet sophisticated, layout, the photo persuades the reader to linger a while. In doing so, the eyes naturally wander to the title and journaling area, where Mindy turned these sketched elements on their side. A small flower crowns the title, adding to the innocent quality of the page.

Supplies: Cardstock (Prism); patterned paper (Dream Street, K&Co., Melissa Frances); brackets (Tinkering Ink); brad, flower, word stickers (Making Memories); adhesive (Therm O Web); Garamond font (Microsoft)

Artwork: Mindy Bush

eye spy

The slightest hint of glitter garnishes the number 2 and the foam circle accents of this page.

I've always wanted to document my asthma on a layout as a reminder I am doing all that I can to maintain control of this disease. A dynamic photo of all of the meds I take each day really drives this point home, and this single photo sketch was ideal for that reason. The white rub-on swirls gusting out of the title represent air—something I don't always get enough of. The unevenly placed letters of the title signify those times when the simple act of breathing is a real effort. Random holes punched in the scalloped border and grid paper mimic the polka dots found in the patterned paper.

Supplies: Cardstock (Bazzill); patterned paper (Sassafras Lass, Scenic Route); chipboard letters (Scenic Route); rub-ons (BasicGrey); letter stickers (KI Memories); acrylic paint (Delta); adhesive (3M, Glue Dots); Teen Light font (Internet download)

A childhood friendship is something to treasure, as Denine details on this all-boy layout. The diagonal lines of the patterned paper on the left immediately pull the eye toward the affable grins of the two subjects, Ryan and his best friend, Devn. The chipboard "2" supports the first word of the title on its cap, then transitions down to strip journaling in a childlike font. A vertical row of embellished asymmetrical circles keeps the mood of the page carefree and happy while staying true to the design of the sketch.

Supplies: Cardstock (Die Cuts With A View); patterned paper (Piggy Tales, Scenic Route); chipboard number, letter stickers (BasicGrey); brads, glitter (Making Memories); foam circles (Fibrecrafts); adhesive (EK Success); Cammi-Pea font (Internet download)

Artwork: Denine Zielinski

Judi has an uncanny ability to mix and match papers and embellishments unlike any other artist I know. In fact, she is fearless about it. This layout is yet another example of that wonderful skill. Although the sketch is quite linear and simple, when interpreted by Judi, it quickly goes over the top with tactile layers and unexpected extras. Even though Judi maintained the design of the sketch, it is when you reach the journaling area that you see a significant, yet pleasant, shift. She placed layer upon layer of cardstock stickers with words and messages that convey the comfort of a cup of coffee. Three-dimensional flowers are positioned in a visual triangle, drawing the eyes to the center of the page.

Supplies: Cardstock (Bazzill); letter and 3D stickers, patterned paper (K&Co.); cardstock stickers (Melissa Frances); word strip stickers (7gypsies); velvet ribbon (May Road); adhesive (Henkel)

Artwork: Judi VanValkinburgh

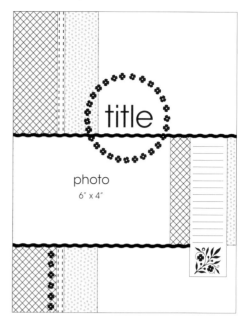

the little moments that make life BIG

The beginning of spring is usually heralded forth with a flourish of color and the awakening of all the flora and fauna. For our family, that includes annual trips to Central Park and the New York Botanical Gardens.

In freestyle fashion, Amy fused together a gorgeous palette of springtime colors to create this outstanding digital layout. Bugs, doodles and swirls frolic around the photos of family and flowers, adding to the carefree theme of the page. Strategically placed drop shadows add depth and dimension to this richly vivid layout, proving that sketches are great for digital artists, too.

Supplies: Image editing software (Adobe); corner swirls, flower and grass doodles, patterned paper from Playful Spring Kit (ScrapArtist); butterflies, dragonfly elements from Fluttering Flourishes Kit (Jen Wilson); scalloped frame from Lime Cordial Kit (Jen Wilson)

Artwork: Amy Goldstein, *Friend of PageMaps*

Because I had more photos than the sketch illustrated, I decided to use the right half of the sketch and place the action photos of Kylie in an accordion book that closes with a magnetic clasp. Woven scraps of patterned paper cover the large chipboard star with glass-beaded wire wrapped around the points. A hand-drawn frame marches around three sides of the page, broken up with small brads and penned dots.

Supplies: Cardstock (WorldWin); patterned paper, ribbon (Stemma); magnetic closure (BasicGrey); letter stickers (American Crafts, Arctic Frog); chipboard; glass beads (Blue Moon, Mill Hill) wire; mini brads (Queen & Co.); acrylic paint (Delta); decorative scissors; pen (American Crafts); adhesive (3M, Glue Dots); Gauntlet Classic font (Internet download)

Photos: Tricia Ribble

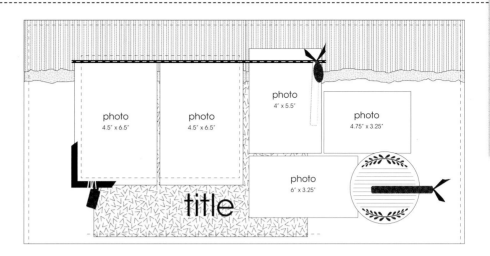

A thin piece of orange cardstock spans the left and right side of the title's descending "P," directing the eye to the remainder of the title on the right side.

Choosing complimentary photos is key when you create a large montage such as the one found on this sketch. Otherwise, the photos have a tendency to compete with one another. Marla struck a nice balance, conveying the crisp, cool autumn season with coordinating patterned paper and an understated, yet visible, title. As her colorful journaling conveys, Liam's search not only resulted in the perfect pumpkin, but a day of wonderful memories for the entire family.

Supplies: Cardstock; patterned paper (Arctic Frog); letter stickers (American Crafts, Making Memories); happy sticker (Arctic Frog); circle sticker (Memories Complete); rub-ons (Fancy Pants); adhesive (3M); American Typewriter font (Microsoft)

Artwork: Marla Kress

Supplies: Cardstock (Prism, WorldWin); patterned paper (BasicGrey, Scenic Route); flowers, word sticker (Cloud 9); letter stickers (Arctic Frog); brads (KI Memories); ink (Ranger); circle punch; adhesive (3L); Georgia font (Microsoft)

Artwork: Tiffany Tillman

After a quick counterclockwise rotation of the sketch, Tiffany squared up the bottom three photos to a more linear position. The focal photo, matted in black, shares rent with a simple, yet bold, title. Three dimensional flower stickers create a visual triangle, drawing the eye to the darling photos of Lita. Dark pink journaling strips offer contrast and tell a delightful story of how Lita transforms into a pajama princess.

Judi's handwritten journaling is the catalyst for this authentic, heartfelt page about her son's autism. She drew inspiration from her photo and kept it the focus of her page by replacing the three smaller photos on the sketch with a large, contrasting title. Descriptive word stickers are scattered throughout, and foam leaf embellishments signify a change of season. A subtitle bisecting the journaling is a reminder that although Eddie is a high-functioning autistic child, Judi's family counts every blessing, both great and small.

Supplies: Cardstock (Bazzill, Prism); patterned paper (Bo-Bunny, Melissa Frances); cardstock stickers (Bazzill); stamps (Art Declassified, Purple Onion); ink (Ranger); epoxy stickers (K&Co.); label sticker (Melissa Frances); foam leaves (Oriental Trading); adhesive (Henkel, Therm O Web, Tombow)

Artwork: Judi VanValkinburgh

I love our tradition of going to Yellowstone National Park for Chris' birthday. Although we go several times throughout the year, I really love the June trip. The Park is alive with spring ... bison and elk calves, trout rising to a caddis hatch, a hint of wild flower blossoms, and a palette of gorgeous green amidst small patches of snow that have not yet given way to the warmer temperatures.

the pride of the park

Some years we make our annual trek in the late spring snow and cold, but this year we were met with a glorious, sunny day, very little traffic on the narrow, antiquated road system, and a small gathering of visitors at Old Faithful. We both commented that it was one of the best eruptions we had ever seen. YNP is a true U.S. treasure and we are so lucky to have it right in our backyard.

Mother Nature lent a hand in the organic theme of this page. A piece of hemp cording frames the layout, held in place with zigzag stitches. I extended the focal photo found on the sketch to show the tremendous height of Old Faithful, and three smaller photos visually support the detailed journaling. The journaling itself is tucked up against an oversized bracket, uniting the story with the photos. A passport stamp was a creative way to display the date of our visit to the park.

Supplies: Cardstock (Bazzill, Paper Company); patterned paper (BasicGrey, Cosmo Cricket); chipboard bracket (Fancy Pants); glass beads (Flair); crackle medium, ink (Ranger); cord, passport stamp, stems, thread (unknown); chalk (Pebbles); adhesive (3M, Glue Dots, Making Memories); Effloresce Antique, P22 Cezanne fonts (Internet download)

tip: When using crackle medium, sometimes the cracks do not show up very well. To emphasize the fractures, rub dark chalk or dye-based ink into the cracks with a makeup sponge.

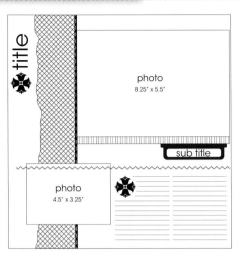

After creating my photo collage, I rotated this sketch counterclockwise to better accommodate the height of the photo. The accent colors introduced on this page are very subdued, despite the fact they are red and black, demonstrating that a modest amount of color goes a long way. The red accents appear in an "L" formation, drawing the eye up to the focal photo and journaling. A black tape label, positioned on a slant, divides the lower third of the page, where descriptive words are printed over paint-covered patterned paper. An elaborate script font, printed directly on the background paper, reverberates the chipboard title.

Supplies: Patterned paper (7gypsies, Cosmo Cricket, Crate Paper); chipboard letters (Crate Paper); metal emblems (K&Co.); label (Dymo); rub-ons (BasicGrey, Daisy D's, My Mind's Eye); fabric tab (Me & My Big Ideas); acrylic paint (Delta); chalk (Pebbles); notebook paper; adhesive (3M, Glue Dots); Beautiful ES, Carbonated Gothic, Stack fonts (Internet downloads); image editing software (Adobe)

tip: How do you combine eight photos onto one page and still maintain continuity? Create a collage photo. Using image-editing software, import all the photos you'd like to include into one file and convert each one to a sepia tone, if desired. Adjust the opacity on each photo (individually) until you are happy with the result. A collage photo invites the reader to study and identify the different images of the photo juxtaposition.

For many of us, pets are essential members of the family and the loss of one is heartbreaking. Denine documents the passing of her furry friend, Miss Kitty, in this engaging, tender layout. The large type of her modest title, created from white letter stickers, captures the eye and calls attention to the focal photo. A drop cap identifies the beginning of Denine's touching journaling directly below. Chipboard accents, positioned on opposite corners of the page, draw the artistic elements together, creating a cohesive look to the entire layout.

Supplies: Cardstock (Bazzill); patterned paper (Cloud 9; K&Co.); chipboard accent (Cloud 9); paw print brads (Sue Zipkin); die-cut border (Doodlebug); rub-on stitches (K&Co.); letter stickers (Reminisce); adhesive (Henkel, Plaid); Wendy Medium, Will & Grace (Internet download)

Artwork: Denine Zielinski

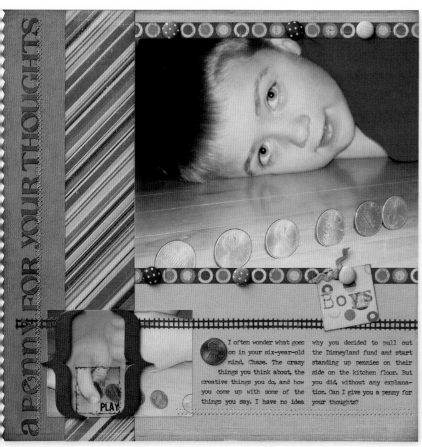

Unlocking the mysteries of a six-year-old's mind has proven to be a daunting task for Chase's mom Tricia, as the journaling on this page reveals. But hey, give the kid props for standing that many pennies up! The smaller, supporting photo pops with the help of a window transparency, framed in two red brackets. Initially, the lengthy, same-sized sticker title looked stranded, but with a quick zigzag stitch, it integrated with the layout. Finally, the left edge of the page is trimmed off with decorative scissors, adding tactile interest.

Supplies: Cardstock, patterned paper, rub-ons, tag (Crate Paper); chipboard, letter stickers (BasicGrey); transparency (Autumn Leaves); acrylic paint, fabric brads, rickrack (Making Memories); decorative scissors; penny; adhesive (3M, Glue Dots); John Doe font (Internet download)

Photos: Tricia Ribble

desert

Liam, it was so cool to finally mee
visited Arizona. I'd been watchin
your mom's scrapbook pages, bu

photo
2.25" x 3.25"

photo
2.25" x 2.25"

photo
2.25" x 2.75"

p

from simple
to savvy

Do you scrapbook in a classic, timeless style? Are your pages contemporary and clean? Are you fond of romantic papers and ornate embellishments? Do your layouts boast a playful, dimensional charm? Do you have panache with a retro, funky flair? No matter your style, sketches can easily be adapted to suit it, from the most clean, trouble-free design to the most complex, forward-thinking techniques. Even if your style changes and grows, you will discover that sketches remain very flexible. In this chapter, we will explore a menagerie of styles and techniques to inspire your next creative endeavor.

Whether you stay within the confines of a sheet of paper or adapt a sketch for other artistic surfaces, I challenge you to let your imagination run wild and step outside of your style comfort zone. Choose what appeals to you. Test a new technique. Try a new color combination. Even if only for a day, be an artistic rebel!

> What great thing would you attempt if you knew you
> could not fail? Robert H. Schuller

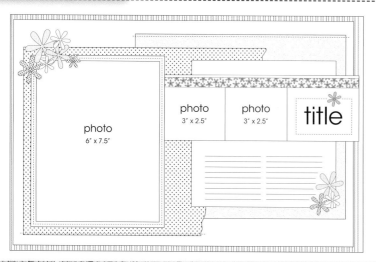

tip: When using fabric (such as heavy denim) to cover chipboard, it is helpful to stiffen the fabric first to reduce fraying and to make the fabric easier to trim.

Fact is stranger than fiction, but I assure you that every one of these Montana claims is true. To accentuate the western ambience of the page, my husband donated an old pair of Wranglers (what a guy!), from which I created denim accents and a frayed mat for the focal photo. The two smaller photos on the sketch were combined into one, allowing more space for my title. The edges of the strip journaling, printed in reverse type, were sanded for an aged, worn effect. Yee-haw!

Supplies: Cardstock (Bazzill, Prism); patterned paper (Adornit, Chatterbox); chipboard letters (BasicGrey); rub-ons (My Mind's Eye); fabric stiffener (Aleene's); denim; adhesive (3M, Glue Dots); Poor Richard font (Internet download)

The 70th year

Seventy years. It is an amount of time that I cannot even begin to imagine. It is a lifetime to some people. It is twice as long as I have even been on this earth, and it is the amount of time that these two people have been together... living, loving, and raising a family. They have laughed. They have cried. They have won. They have lost. Together, my grandparents have watched the world evolve from the early days of television to the information super highway. Many things have changed in their seventy years of marriage, but one thing has not. Their love is stronger now than ever. It is amazing to see and feel the love that these two people share with each other even after all of their years together. They are amazing. They are beautiful. They are a testament to the power of love.

Leonard & Mary Blihar

Denine commemorates the (astounding) 70th wedding anniversary of her grandparents in this romantic layout. Using only three photos, she captured the essence of their enduring love, and that theme is unmistakable throughout the two-page spread. After switching the title area with its neighboring photo, Denine created a striking caption that unites the two supporting photos. Carefree hearts in coordinating colors cavort about the page, framing both the focal photo and hugging the corner of her heartfelt journaling.

Supplies: Cardstock (Bazzill); patterned paper (Autumn Leaves, BasicGrey); chipboard numbers and elements, letter stickers (BasicGrey); dimensional sticker (K&Co.); die-cut hearts (Provo Craft); slot punching tool (Making Memories); ink (Clearsnap); adhesive (EK Success); Times New Roman font (Microsoft)

Artwork: Denine Zielinski

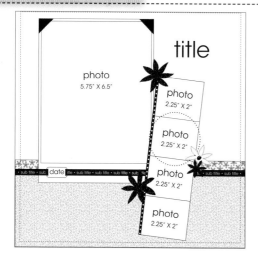

tip: To achieve the tie-dye effect of this title, soak crumpled chunks of tissue paper in equal parts of glue and water and press firmly to the back of transparent letters. While wet, dab multiple watercolors into the tissue paper with a sponge or paint brush. After the letters are dry, carefully trim excess tissue paper with a craft knife.

Hang ten, baby! These action photos of Chase soaring down a super slide went perfectly with the filmstrip style of the sketch. The story of this daredevil boy's voyage down the larger-than-life water slide is hidden behind the filmstrip, hinged closed with a photo anchor. Chipboard splashes, covered in ultra thick embossing enamel, hug each side, adding a watery texture to the page.

Supplies: Cardstock (Bazzill); patterned paper (Scenic Route); clear letters (Heidi Swapp); rub-ons (BasicGrey, My Mind's Eye); chipboard swirls (Fancy Pants); glass pebbles (Robin's Nest); ink (Ranger, Versamark); adhesive (3M, Aleene's); tissue paper; Ultra Thick Embossing Enamel; Tork font (Internet download)

Photos: Tricia Ribble

A childhood board game turned out to be the inspiration for Patti's playful page. Mimicking the colors of the game, she layered punched circles and numbered stickers on the patterned paper in coordinating colors. Patti corralled her title in a circle of painted dots, repeating the geometric shapes found in the lower third of the page. A starburst shape serves as a closure and, when rotated, the photo strip pops opens to reveal colorful journaling about Alex's strategy for beating his mom at the game. A red stitched border, creatively interrupted with stamped words from the game, frames the entire layout. Now does this cute kid look like he's sorry?

Supplies: Cardstock (Bazzill); patterned paper (American Crafts, Arctic Frog); letter stickers (American Crafts, Arctic Frog, Making Memories); chipboard (Cactus Pink); decorative punches; letter stamps (Karen Foster); ink (Clearsnap); fasteners (All My Memories); thread; adhesive (Xyron); Garamond font (Microsoft

Artwork: Patti Milazzo, *Friend of PageMaps*

Boys may be made of snakes, snails and puppy dog tails. But in the desert, it is all about the geckos, something that fascinated Liam on his Phoenix vacation. A dimensional, hand-cut lizard (held in place with dimensional adhesive) crawls up the center of the page, surrounded by photos of Sonoran flora and one adorable boy. Chipboard covered in sandstone texture anchors two photos, drawing the eye to the center of the page. This sketch is perfect when you have small, non-competing pictures to support a focal photo.

Supplies: Cardstock, brads (Bazzill); patterned paper (Tinkering Ink); rub-on numbers (BasicGrey); sandstone texture (DecoArt); glitter; acrylic paint (Delta, Junkitz); decorative scissors; adhesive (3M, EK Success); lizard (artist's own design); Rock It, Susanna fonts (Internet download)

Photo: Marla Kress

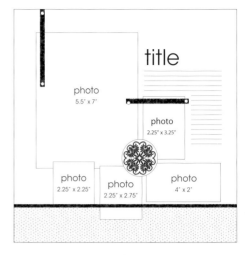

Need brads but can't find the right color? Paint them, as I did on this page, for a perfect match!

Hey, if you can't laugh at yourself, who can you laugh at? This absurd page is a good case in point. I rotated the sketch counterclockwise and created a vertical chipboard film strip to house a set of mini photos. Now take one look at that silly main photo—you can't help but want to read the amusing story of how I could have possibly wanted that photo taken! A path is torn through the center of the vellum journaling block, where I tucked in my title. You know, I really am a dork.

Supplies: Cardstock (Bazzill); patterned paper (Bo-Bunny, Dream Street, Imaginisce); parchment vellum (Prism); letter stickers (Bo-Bunny); plastic tag (Pebbles); rub-ons (American Crafts); chipboard, ribbon (unknown); adhesive (3M, Glue Dots); Apple Garamond font (Internet download)

Photo: Amy Goldstein

An amazing photographer in her own right, Mindy has a wide assortment of photos at her disposal (she's a mother of six!). However, finding eight coordinating color photos of her son, Dallen, proved difficult so she converted a series of her favorites to black and white. Mindy squared up the photos and elements of the sketch to better suit her linear style. An oversized number 5 guides the eye to Mindy's journaling, where "you make me laugh" is fully authenticated by the giggling photos of her adorable son.

Supplies: Cardstock (Prism); letter stickers, patterned paper (American Crafts); ribbon (Stemma); number sticker (Making Memories); rub-ons (K&Co.); vellum; adhesive (Therm O Web); Chanl font (Internet download)

Artwork: Mindy Bush

eye (spy)

Mindy printed her journaling on vellum, showing a subtle hint of the patterned paper underneath.

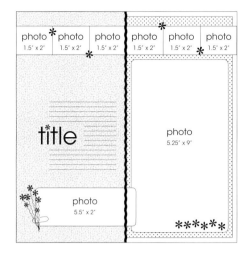

"Wow" was the first word out of my mouth when Judi sent me this layout, and her amazing photography is just the start to this wonderful page. I think it is one of those unique pieces of art that encourages a reader to linger a while and uncover the multitude of watery, fluid details. From the inclusion of her family's season pass ticket to the glass-like buttons that adorn the bottom right corner, this layout packs a powerful punch.

Supplies: Cardstock (Prism); patterned paper (Urban Lily); transparency (Hambly); acrylic letters (KI Memories); chipboard word (K&Co.); bracket brads (Around the Block); chipboard numbers, ribbon (Maya Road); acrylic paint, glossy accents, ink (Ranger); buttons (Autumn Leaves); floss; ultra thick embossing enamel; adhesive (Henkel, Therm O Web); Andale Mono font (Internet download)

Artwork: Judi VanValkinburgh

give it a try

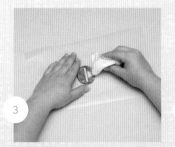

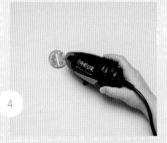

1. Paint raw chipboard a coordinating color and allow to dry.

2. Apply a thin coat of embossing ink to the surface.

3. Sprinkle on ultra thick embossing enamel (UTEE). Shake off the excess and let a few areas remain uncovered.

4. Melt with heat gun. (Don't let the tip of the heat gun get too close to the painted chipboard or the paint will bubble.)

fly fishing with Sean Connery (well, sorta)

catch of the day

As if fly fishing in New Zealand wasn't cool enough, hangin' with Sean Connery for three days really topped the trip! [OK, get real Fleck.] But man, it was freaky how much this dude looked and sounded like Agent 007, hence the ring of numbers and stitches that group two of our photos together. The subtitle is made up of printed strips of paper, folded in half, and sewn onto the bottom border. This sketch is perfect when you have fewer photos of a stellar event. Oh, and yes, that is a real trout—all five and a half pounds of him!

Supplies: Cardstock (Prism); patterned paper (Dream Street, Scribble Scrabble); die-cut numbers (QuicKutz); ink (Ranger); thread; adhesive (3M); Establo, Gauntlet Classic, Pea Jenny fonts (Internet download)

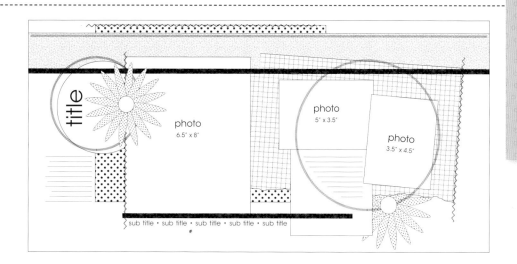

No one thinks outside the creative box quite like my friend Marla. There have been countless times I've wanted to share her brain for a few days, just to recharge my mojo. This layout is a great example of her artistic originality. A number of notable elements immediately jump off this page: a bold, eye-catching title, hand-embroidered floral accents, and a photo of a children's book spine that serves as the subtitle found on the sketch. However, the layout's pièce de résistance is the letter sticker circle that encompasses the two photos on the right side. What a cool idea!

Supplies: Cardstock (Bazzill, Prism); patterned paper (Crate Paper); felt flowers (Prima); letter stickers (American Crafts, Arctic Frog); chipboard (Maya Road); paint, floss (Making Memories); adhesive (3M); Dear Joe II font (Internet download)

Artwork: Marla Kress

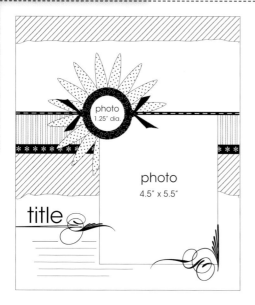

My grandmother taught me how to embroider at a young age so it was only fitting that I pay tribute to this age-old craft by creating a page about her, adorned in silk-embroidered designs. Although paper is not as forgiving as cloth, with a bit of patience and a good paper piercer, the results are extraordinary. Tendrils of petals, leaves and beads surround a heartfelt list of fond memories of my grandmother, and a satin magnolia blossom crowns the top of the page, taking the place of the second circular photo on the sketch.

Supplies: Cardstock (Bazzill); patterned paper, rub-ons (K&Co.); ribbon (Offray, Plaid); pearl brad (Imaginisce); glass beads (Mill Hill); floss (DMC); adhesive (3M); Caslon Swash, Pegsanna HMK fonts (Internet downloads)

After rotating and converting the sketch to her favorite 12" x 12" (30cm x 30cm) format, the elements of Kim's page came together beautifully in a whimsical, freestyle fashion. A title built from various rub-on words border the top and bottom of her photo, and heartfelt motherly advice rests between two brackets. The punch of yellow brings sunshine to the page and a hand-drawn frame ties all the elements together.

Supplies: Cardstock (Bazzill); patterned paper (Tinkering Ink); ribbon (May Arts); flower (Michaels); rub-on (Daisy D's); adhesive (EK Success)

Artwork: Kim Kesti

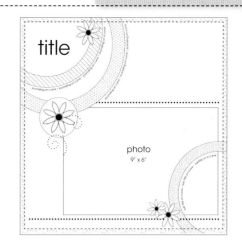

Typing on a curve can be tricky, especially on multiple layers. But with a bit of practice and some patience, success can be achieved. A great alternative would be to handwrite the journaling or to even use stamps or rub-ons. I chose to fill the journaling rings on this sketch with single word attributes about myself. Because I added additional lines of circular text, I moved the title to the right where there was more breathing room. A van Gogh quote, printed directly on the photo, succinctly sums up the journaling. Clusters of clear and tinted plastic flowers randomly embellish the page.

Supplies: Cardstock (Bazzill); die-cut borders, patterned paper (Crate Paper); rub-ons (American Crafts, BasicGrey, Scrapworks); velvet brads (Making Memories); chipboard letters (Pressed Petals); swirl stamp (Gel-à-tins); ink (VersaMark); acrylic paint (Delta); acrylic flowers (KI Memories); plastic flowers (Heidi Swapp, Maya Road); adhesive (3M, Glue Dots); Prissy Frat Boy font (Internet download)

Photo: Amy Goldstein

tip: Clear embellishments are very popular, but often do not show up well against patterned paper. To make the clear plastic flowers on this page pop out, white rub-on designs were applied to the back of each flower. The rub-ons also help disguise the adhesive used to attach them.

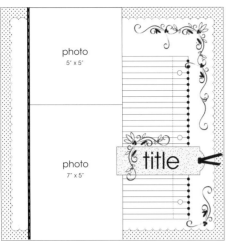

This layout appears disjointed at first glance. Upon reading the candid journaling, it becomes clear why I felt it was essential to cut and reassemble the large photo of my church in such an erratic way. The foundation of the sketch is solid and linear, providing balance and contrast against the chaos of the photo and title I chose to create. The hand-cut flower, resting in the lower right corner softens the page and imparts hope that something misplaced can someday be found.

Supplies: Patterned paper (Scrapworks, Stemma, Webster's Pages); rub-on letters (Delish Designs); rub-on words (Daisy D's); puzzle pieces (Scrapworks); ink (Ranger); adhesive (3M); Apple Garamond (Internet download)

Our church was a big part of my life after we moved back to Montana. I was a Sunday school teacher, a deacon and a member of the choir. I counseled at church camp and cooked one summer. I made home visits with our minister, prepared the weekly bulletin, and even sang a solo a few times. For me, Sunday services were the beginning of my week, not the end. As Pam's cancer progressed, my faith began to wane. I silently cursed God, wondering how He could let such an insidious disease take the life of my very best friend. When Pam's breast cancer metastasized to her brain and I knew she was losing her courageous battle, I stopped attending church. It was rebellious on my part, but I was just so angry and frustrated.

Since her death in August 2006, I've set foot inside our sanctuary one time. Feeling hypocritical and out of place in a home that once brought me comfort and solace, I still haven't managed to find the courage and forgiveness within myself and return to a place I once loved with all my heart.

As seen on the sketch, a playful, scalloped border hugs this page, enhanced with an outline of whimsical dots. The dotted theme carries through to the title and flower border with the help of a polka-dot stamp and glitter-infused embossing powder. Journaling with a hand-scripted font adds to the pixy-like theme, where it rests above and below the contrasting title. Of course, two adorable shots of Denine's niece, Emily, carry the rest of the page.

Supplies: Cardstock (Bazzill); patterned paper (BasicGrey, Making Memories, One Heart); chipboard letters (Delish Designs); letter stickers (American Crafts); brads, glitter, metal tag (Making Memories); die-cut tag (Collage Press); die-cut border (Doodlebug); ink (Clearsnap); stamp (Savvy Stamps); embossing enamel (Ranger); adhesive (EK Success)

Artwork: Denine Zielinski

I'll be the first to admit that we're not raising the brightest puppy. But what Darby lacks in intelligence, she makes up for in endearing qualities. A lifetime friendship—forged in trust (and perhaps just a wee bit of fear on the puppy's part)—is humorously captured in the notebook-style journaling on this "cat-loves-dog" page. A playful bundle of yarn gathered at the bottom right corner of the layout replaces the swirl embellishments found on the sketch and reinforces the feline-canine theme.

Supplies: Cardstock, patterned paper, rub-ons (KI Memories); vellum (Prism); floss (DMC); circle cutter; fabric stiffener (Plaid); notebook paper; twill; adhesive (3M, Glue Dots)

tip: Do you have a great photo but it has a distracting background? Cover it with vellum and cut out a hole to accent the portion of the photo you wish to emphasize.

A six-photo collage, like the one found on this sketch, has no problem competing for attention when each photo is mounted on a contrasting background and separated by equal distances (think of it as tiling with photos). A winding trail of hand-embroidered chicken footprints takes the eye on a journey across the collection of photos, where it rests at the journaling block. A torn fabric strip divides the title from the journaling and adds a bit of country charm.

Supplies: Cardstock (Bazzill, Canson); patterned paper (My Mind's Eye, Time Flies); plastic letters (Maya Road); letter stickers (BasicGrey); fabric strips (Weavewerks); Petal Porcelain (Plaid); Glossy Accents, ink (Ranger); floss (DMC); adhesive (3M, Glue Dots); Footlight MT font (Microsoft)

give it a try

1 Follow the directions on the fabric stiffener and spread wet fabric out on a piece of waxed paper, flattening it with your fingers. Allow to completely dry, turning the fabric over occasionally.

2 Place dry fabric between two pieces of paper and iron on a low setting to press out any wrinkles.

3 Using a clear, liquid adhesive (Ranger Glossy Accents or KI Memories Gloo works great), evenly spread a thin coat of adhesive on the back of the plastic letter and press firmly onto front of stiffened fabric. Work out any air bubbles by pressing your fingers towards the edges.

4 Once dry, trim away excess fabric with a craft knife.

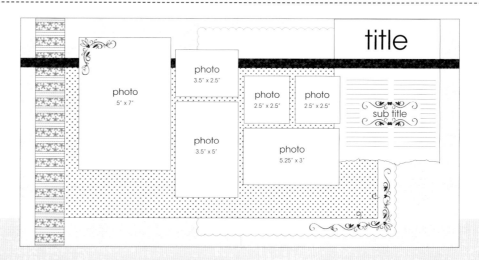

Drenched in a palette of soft, light hues, Chesa the cat stands out front and center. Monochromatic photos such as these work great in a grouping, where one photo doesn't compete with the others. Accents of warm pink highlight the shirt Lita is wearing and the entire layout is united in a background of soft gray. Tiffany chose to break her title into two parts, bringing focus to the center collage of photos.

Supplies: Cardstock (Prism, WorldWin); patterned paper (BasicGrey, K&Co.); frame, title letters (Making Memories); stickers (Sandylion); decorative punch; adhesive (3L); Georgia font (Microsoft)

Artwork: Tiffany Tillman

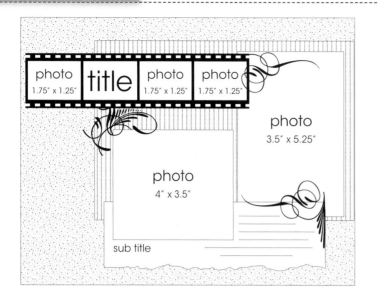

Sandy beach photos can often be challenging to scrapbook, but a neutral background will quickly tame your shots. Picking up accent colors from the photos and using them in small amounts did not detract from Chase and Kylie's fun in the sun, but added punches of color to the layout. All the elements rest on a broad base of swirly black, making the colors on the page pop. A two-toned vertical title and handwritten journaling add to the playfulness of the theme.

Supplies: Cardstock (Bazzill, Prism); patterned paper (Chatterbox, Creative Imaginations); chipboard letters (Scenic Route); mini brads (Queen & Co.); ink (Ranger); adhesive (3M, KI Memories)

Photos: Tricia Ribble

Scrapping everyday moments is definitely Judi's bag and there is no doubt she had fun creating this page! Judi abandoned the row of small photos in favor of a larger title, anchored with chipboard tiles that emphasize the subject of her page. Her journaling (handwritten directly over the photo), explains why Eddie is grinning from ear to ear. Rub-on words function as oversized photo corners, defining the qualities of most little boys.

Supplies: Cardstock (Prism); patterned paper, rub-ons (Daisy D's); chipboard tiles (Urban Lily); chipboard letters (American Crafts); transparency; letter and word stickers (EK Success); embossing ink, paint (Ranger); ultra thick embossing enamel; adhesive (Henkel, Therm O Web, Tombow)

Artwork: Judi VanValkinburgh

tip: Preprinted embellishments can be altered easily. Judi placed a white sticker over the word "me" and replaced it with "you" on her chipboard tile.

The last thing that we expected to find in the Arizona desert was a safari adventure. But "Out of Africa" was just that. You were amazed by the animals and just how closely we could see them. And quite frankly, so were we!

With an unobtrusive background pattern, Marla had the freedom to use bold accent colors in her title and subtitle, which is broken into two parts as shown on the sketch. The blue and orange really pop off the page, accentuating those same colors found in her close-up photos. A strip of sandpaper placed across the top echoes the desert theme of the page.

Supplies: Cardstock (Prism); patterned paper (Adornit, Dream Street); letter stickers (BasicGrey, Making Memories,); sandpaper; adhesive (3M); Geneva font (Microsoft)

Artwork: Marla Kress

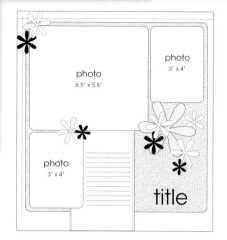

Simple does not mean boring when it comes to scrapbooking. Strong photographs, a good choice of patterned paper and minimal accents make for a savvy, yet simple page. All the elements of the sketch were achieved with little fuss and this page was completed in no time at all.

Supplies: Cardstock, brads (Bazzill); letter stickers, patterned paper, (BasicGrey); plastic flowers (Heidi Swapp); rub-ons (Fontwerks, K&Co.); ink (Ranger); acrylic paint (Delta); corner rounder; adhesive (3M); Pea Jenny font (Internet download)

tip: When using clear embellishments, try dabbing paint or permanent ink on the edges to help them stand out.

To take the embellishments a few steps further, I replaced the rub-on stitches with a zigzag machine stitch. I then added white rub-ons to the backs of the clear flower accents to help them stand out, and replaced the mini brads with large fabric brads for added texture. I used a few zigzag stitches to attach the clear embellishments, and a combination of matching trim and a chipboard bookplate span the bottom of the focal photo.

Supplies: Cardstock (Bazzill); chipboard, letter stickers, patterned paper (BasicGrey); plastic flowers (Heidi Swapp); rub-ons (BasicGrey, K&Co.); ink (Ranger); acrylic paint (Delta); corner rounder; fabric brads (Imaginisce); trim (Offray); thread; adhesive (3M, Glue Dots); Pea Jenny font (Internet download)

For some added oomph, I substituted the zigzag stitch with multiple rows of single machine stitches in two coordinating thread colors. Using a gloss medium, I beaded the tops of large metal brads for the flower centers and encrusted one clear flower accent with glass and micro beads. I added pen doodling around the flowers and a few rub-ons to the photos, giving an embellished boost to the entire page.

Supplies: Cardstock, brads (Bazzill); chipboard, letter stickers, patterned paper, rub-ons (BasicGrey); plastic flowers (Heidi Swapp); brads (Li'l Davis); glass beads (Darice, Mill Hill); gloss accent, ink (Ranger); acrylic paint (Delta); corner rounder; trim (Offray); thread; adhesive (3M, EK Success, Glue Dots); Pea Jenny font (Internet download)

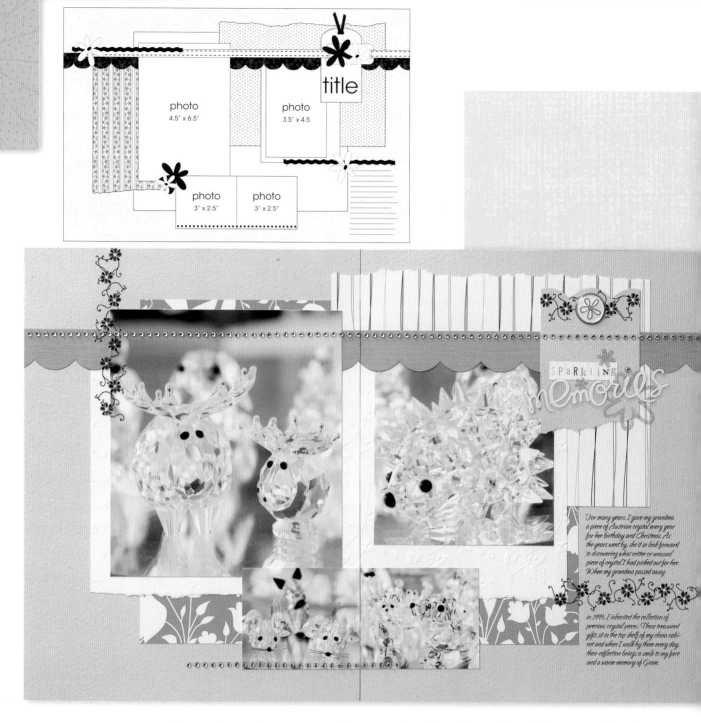

Treasured memories are captured in a page abundant with sparkle and shine, not only in the twinkling photos, but in the accents as well. An understated background of pale blue provides great contrast, while hints of pink and green found in the facets of the crystal, repeat in small layers on the page. A row of rhinestones that runs the full width of the top of the page, replaces the ribbon embellishment found on the sketch. They were the perfect touch for this bling-bling page that pays homage to my grandmother's treasured collection of Austrian crystal.

Supplies: Cardstock (Bazzill, Paper Company); patterned paper (American Crafts); letter stickers, glitter stickers (Making Memories); rub-ons (Polar Bear Press); plastic word, rhinestones (Heidi Swapp); large snap (We R Memory Keepers); glitter (Melissa Frances); adhesive (3M, Glue Dots); Sandy Text font (Hallmark)

Documenting Lita's panache for little girl couture brought Tiffany to the realization that contrast does exist between daughter and mom. As mom admits, sweatpants and sneakers are just her style, where Lita's taste runs more to hip fashion and accessories. Defeated, Tiffany shares her thoughts about this in a journaling block that moved to the left when she flipped the sketch horizontally. A clothing tag from Lita's new outfit is the perfect embellishment.

Supplies: Cardstock (Prism, WorldWin); patterned paper (BasicGrey, Making Memories, Scenic Route); flowers, frame (Daisy D's); tag (Making Memories); decorative punch; stickers (Designer Digitals); shopping tag (Gymboree); adhesive (3L, EK Success); Futura font (Microsoft)

Artwork: Tiffany Tillman

tip: Look beyond store-bought embellishments and incorporate "found objects" into your page as Tiffany did here by using a clothing tag.

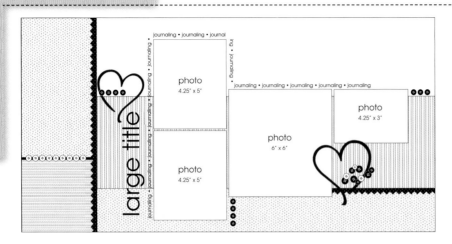

Coastal colors complement the seaside theme of this layout without overwhelming the photos. With such a lengthy title, I decided to shift it to the upper left corner. I painted the chipboard letters white and paint-spattered them with complementary colors. After inking the top and bottom edges of each letter, I stacked the words on their side. A photo corner turned on its point signifies the start of the journaling that wraps around the top half of the photos.

Supplies: Cardstock, acrylic buttons (Bazzill); patterned paper (Crate Paper, Making Memories, Wübe); chipboard letters (BasicGrey); acrylic buckle (KI Memories); date tabs (Martha Stewart); acrylic paint (Delta); photo corners, ribbon (Making Memories); floss (DMC); ink (Ranger); decorative scissors; thread; adhesive (3M, KI Memories); Avant Garde (Microsoft)

Photos: Chris Fleck

tip: Backing acrylic embellishments with patterned paper is a cinch, as I did on a set of oversized, clear buttons. Using a clear adhesive, apply a thin, even coat to the back of a button and place it on the paper. Apply even pressure for several seconds to release any air bubbles. Once dry, trim off excess paper.

A 12" x 12" (30cm x 30cm) double sketch turned on its side makes for one impressive, tall layout. With an affection for calendars (she has four on her desk!), Judi used this new found length to her advantage, incorporating a family calendar into the page. Her daily routine is recorded on small to-do lists, supported with random photos of weekly happenings. A humorous title in mixed-media letters keeps the mood light.

Supplies: Cardstock (Bazzill, Prism); patterned paper (Scenic Route); chipboard accents (American Crafts, K&Co., Li'l Davis, Pressed Petals, Scenic Route, We R Memory Keepers); metal "E" (Making Memories); stickers (7gypsies); calendar page (Board Dudes); rickrack; notebook to-do lists

Artwork: Judi VanValkinburgh

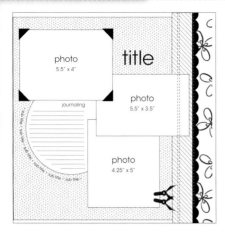

Supplies: Cardstock (Bazzill); patterned paper (Crate Paper); transparency (Hambly); circle stickers (Memories Complete); decorative tape (7gypsies); number stickers (American Crafts, Scenic Route); adhesive (3M); LHF Sophia Script, Skia fonts (Internet downloads)

Artwork: Marla Kress

tip: To create a look like Marla's, begin by creating your full page first, adhering all paper and photo layers together. Then trim the journaling circle. You'll get a much cleaner edge that way. Also, most preprinted transparencies are not ink-jet or laser print ready. To add journaling, print it on a separate piece of transparency and adhere the piece underneath the decorative transparency that fills the partial circle.

In striking contrast to the opaque nature of the patterned paper, Marla incorporated a piece of printed transparency in place of the paper strip illustrated on the sketch. Continuing her transparent theme, she also used another piece to house her journaling, wrapping the text around the preprinted floral elements. Can you say "Wow!"? A unique layout like this looks best standing on an easel in your home, not tucked away in a scrapbook album.

Quiet whispers of pastel colors capture the essence of this soft page, allowing the photos to take center stage. A mother's straight-from-the-heart journaling required little more than a gentle, script font set in a quarter circle as seen on the sketch. Tiny flowers made from felt ribbon, sequins and a brad are tucked around the corners of the photos, drawing the eye to the center of the page.

Supplies: Cardstock (Bazzill); patterned paper (Delish Designs, Melissa Frances); letter stickers (Making Memories); felt flowers, mini brads (Queen & Co.); flower jewels (Heidi Swapp); sequins (Doodlebug, Queen & Co.); decorative scissors; adhesive (3M); Lindy font (Internet download)

Photos: Tricia Ribble

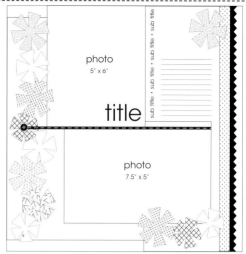

A page teaming with western flair is most deserving of a unique title, especially when it features such an adorable cowgirl! I soaked cotton floss in fabric stiffener, then wrapped it around a long length of thin wire. Once dry, I was able to shape the covered wire into the words of the title, ending it with a lasso around a denim flower. Irregular cross-stitches on both photos and sewn buttons boost the handmade theme of the page.

Supplies: Cardstock (Bazzill); patterned paper (Chatterbox); thread (DMC); wire (Making Memories); fabric stiffener (Plaid); ink (Ranger); buttons (Bazzill, Melissa Frances); die-cut (Sizzix); denim; adhesive (3M, Glue Dots); Poor Richard font (Internet download)

Photos: Marla Kress

Using playful tween papers in vibrant, youthful colors, Denine did not want the patterns to overwhelm the wonderful photos of her son Ryan and his good friend Deanna. To escape this problem, she converted her crisp, sharp photos to black and white, causing them to pop right off the page. Assorted-sized paper circles, embellished with oversized grommets, cascade down the left side of the page, adding interest to this energized layout. Small lengths of ribbon, folded in half, pinch-hit for "pseudo" leaves on the flowerlike orbs. Hints of contrasting black cardstock unify the black-and-white photos, all resulting in one fantastic layout.

Supplies: Cardstock (Bazzill); patterned paper (Chatterbox, Imaginisce); die-cut letters (QuicKutz, Sizzix); grommets, slot punching tool, brads (Making Memories); ink (Clearsnap); circle punch; ribbon (Shoebox Trims); Times New Roman font (Microsoft)

Artwork: Denine Zielinski

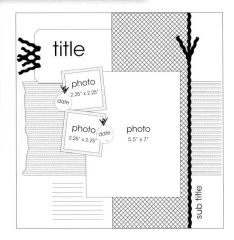

Mindy rotated this sketch 180° to better suit the direction her darling daughter was facing in the main photo. She replaced the two small supporting photos with windows, trimmed two small slits between the squares with an craft knife, then thread a broad length of ribbon through the squares. A curvy edge to the patterned paper on the left gives a soft, feminine look to the page.

Supplies: Cardstock (Prism); patterned paper (Melissa Frances); ribbon (Martha Stewart); circle and scallop cutter, flower (Making Memories); square punch; adhesive (Ad Tech); Doctor, Gauntlet Thin fonts (Internet downloads)

Artwork: Mindy Bush

I wanted to pay tribute to my best friend of twenty-three years with more than just a scrapbook page. The frame and sketch perfectly suited one another, and now I have a lasting memory that greets me on my desk each day. Glass beads sewn to the background accentuate the flowers within the patterned paper and the beaded theme carries over to the exterior photo. Angel wings edged in glitter add a touch of whimsy and serve as a reminder that Pam is now my angel from above.

Supplies: Frame (Creative Imaginations); embossed cardstock (Doodlebug); patterned paper (Fancy Pants); acrylic paint (Delta); rub-ons (BasicGrey); clear letters (Heidi Swapp); dimensional paint, ink (Ranger); glitter (Melissa Frances); glass beads (Mill Hill); adhesive (3M, Beacon); Apple Garamond font (Internet download), LT Zapfino font (Microsoft)

When my husband discovered me taking photographs of the remote controls in our house, he looked at me as if I had three heads. "But wait!" I said, "I have this really cool idea for the last page of the book!" The "pause" theme came to life and afforded me the perfect opportunity to thank friends and manufacturers for their time, talent and generosity in the making of this book.

More importantly, I owe a big thank you to you, the reader. I hope you have found inspiration and motivating ideas within these pages. Please turn the page to learn more about the talented contributors and generous manufacturers who helped bring this book to life.

Supplies: Cardstock (Bazzill); patterned paper, rub-ons (BasicGrey); rub-on letters (Arctic Frog); ink (Ranger); metal tag, ribbon (Making Memories); decorative scissors; thread; adhesive (3M, Glue Dots); ArriereGarde font (Internet download); Avant Garde font (Microsoft)

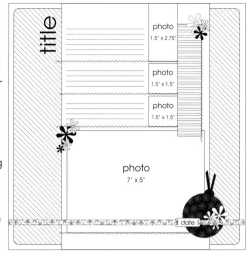

beckyfleck

This is me, in a nutshell. I am an illustrator by trade, but quickly discovered that I would starve had I chosen that career path. I totally dig my job at BasicGrey, where I am the chief bottle washer and creative something or other, depending on the day of the week. I love to teach scrapbooking and once convinced a student in Edmonton that I was Brad Pitt's ex-wife. I answer to Fleck, Fleckster, Fleckinator and Vern. Call me Rebecca and I'll have to hurt you. I am snarky. A fly fishing guide once told me I have Tourette's Syndrome when I catch a fish (great visual on that, eh?). All of my children have four legs and fur. My latest goal is to get a tattoo on LA Ink. I fly by the seat of my pants because my mom gave me courage and high-tech wings.

Supplies: Image editing software (Adobe); ruler brush by Kellie Mize (Measured Edges); circle brush, graph label, number stamps, paper by Rhonna Farrer (Two Peas in a Bucket); maple leaf (Microsoft); 321 Impact, Carbonated Gothic fonts (Internet downloads)

Photo: Chris Fleck

marlakress

If I were to make a list of all the qualities I'd want in a best friend, Marla fits the bill to the tee. She has been my cheerleader, crying towel, advice giver, keeper of secrets, motivator and all-around great friend for many years. Marla is benevolent, giving, caring and funny, and (politely) laughs at all my silly jokes and quips. Best of all, she's the most talented scrapbooker I know, and all the wonderful qualities she possesses come through in her work. Every page she created for this book left me asking myself, "Why didn't I think of that?" Her creativity ticks on a level I can't even begin to wrap my head around. Marla loves the heat of Arizona (crazy, but true), although she lives in the cold of Cheswick, Pennsylvania, with her husband and two beautiful children, Liam and Adeline.

Supplies: Cardstock (Bazzill); letter stickers, patterned paper (American Crafts); chipboard (Urban Lily); sticker (7gypsies); adhesive (3M); Georgia font (Microsoft)

Artwork: Marla Kress

The most important, wonderful things in my life are captured by my camera. Beautiful smiles, hugs, kisses and moments of time I want to remember forever. I'm glad I have a lifetime to take photos of my family.

me

mindybush

Mindy is one of the most talented photographers I know and it is readily apparent in all of her work. Her style is contemporary and simple and her pages are captivating and engaging, both in substance and in photos. She flawlessly converted each of the sketches she worked on to fit her unique, linear style. Mindy is also quite talented in using Photoshop actions to enhance and repair even the most problematic photo. Mindy lives in Ammon, Idaho, with her husband and six children.

Supplies: Cardstock (Prism); patterned paper (Heidi Grace, KI Memories); embossed paper (Lasting Impressions); flower, ribbon (Martha Stewart); letter stickers (Making Memories); adhesive (Tombow); Bodoni font (Microsoft)

Artwork: Mindy Bush

tiffanytillman

Spend just a few minutes on the phone with Tiffany and your sides will ache from laughter. She has an extraordinary sense of humor, loves *Beavis and Butthead* (a quality quite endearing to me), watches SportsCenter religiously (how can you not love this gal?) and is a truly gifted scrapbooker. Her philosophy for recording history through her pages is to touch on the very heart of the subject, and she does so through authentic, honest and sometimes very funny journaling. Tiffany lives in Virginia Beach, Virginia, with her husband and darling daughter, Carmelita.

Supplies: Cardstock (WorldWin); patterned paper (American Crafts); chipboard letters (Zsiage); brads (Imaginisce); ink (Ranger); circle punch; adhesive (3L); Futura Md BT font (Microsoft)

Artwork: Tiffany Tillman

judivanvalkinburgh

I first discovered Judi through her altered artwork and was quite literally taken back with her unique, exceptional style. I now fondly refer to her as the quintessential renaissance woman of scrapbooking and altered art. I don't know many artists who can take no less than ten manufacturer's products, pull them all together, and make a project look so darn good. I'm telling you, she could make a tissue box look like a work of art! Judi designs for multiple manufacturers and lives in Niagara Falls, New York, with her husband and five children.

Supplies: Patterned paper (K&Co., Scenic Route); rub-on letters (American Crafts); brads, decorative tape, felt flowers (Making Memories); ghost letters (Heidi Swapp); velvet flowers (Maya Road); chipboard brackets (We R Memory Keepers); tag (7gypsies); ink (StazOn); adhesive (Henkel, Tombow)

Artwork: Judi VanValkinburgh

deninezielinski

At first glance of her work, you might consider Denine to be a simple scrapbooker. But look closely and you will discover hidden nuggets of details—rich with creativity and ingenuity—in every one of her pages. Denine and I met almost four years ago when we both joined the same design team. Since then, we have forged a friendship that has stood the test of time, temper tantrums and unyielding deadlines. I finally met her (in person) at the Craft & Hobby Association's (CHA) annual convention three years ago. She ran into the booth I was working in, planted a big ol' kiss on my cheek, and literally squeezed the stuffing right out of me with a hug. I knew right then she was a keeper. Denine is a special ed teacher who lives in Nanticoke, Pennsylvania, with her adorable son Ryan.

Supplies: Cardstock (Bazzill, Diecuts With A View); patterned paper (Imaginisce); die-cut letters (Sizzix); brads (Making Memories); rub-on number (Doodlebug); adhesive (EK Success)

Artwork: Denine Zielinski

friends of PaGeMaps

patti milazzo
becky heisler
connie peterlanjes
amy goldstein
kim kesti
sheredian vickers
vicki harvey
dawn inskip
shawna martinez

Nine super talented artists have contributed beautiful sketch samples throughout this book. Not only are are they my friends, they are great friends to PageMaps!

A girl couldn't ask for nine better friends than this group of talented scrapbookers. Together, these amazing artists created some fantastic pages for this book.

Shawna (my home girl and tried-and-true friend) gives me a daily dose of snark and laughter, although I have to be careful not to drink Diet Coke and read her blog at the same time!

I have Amy to thank for helping me improve my photography skills (such as they are), although I still call her regularly about my camera settings. She's a wonderful digi artist and loves lime green.

Dawn is my sweet tart across the pond who forever amazes me with her layering techniques.

Kim is a terrific artist from Arizona, and I often wonder how she gets such great scrapbooking done with seven little ones under foot!

Patt-ay has an abundance of design savvy and is truly killer with a sewing machine.

Becky is my go-to bud who will bail me out of a PageMaps newsletter pinch on very short notice, and does so with a knock-out page.

Sheredian is a "scrap from the heart" kind of gal and I just love her eye for color combinations.

Vicki has a classic, contemporary style that I never get tired of looking at, and she is the creative director at Mustard Moon.

Connie is an undiscovered bundle of talent that, quite honestly, the magazines should be paying much more attention to.

Supplies: Cardstock (Bazzill); patterned paper (BasicGrey, Creative Imaginations); letter stickers (BasicGrey); snaps (Chatterbox); paper flowers (Making Memories); mini brads (Queen & Co.); corner rounder; circle scissors (EK Success); ink (Ranger); adhesive (3M, Glue Dots); AvantGarde font (Microsoft); Qlassik Medium ITC, Pea Jenny fonts (Internet downloads)

sourceguide

The following companies manufacture products featured in this book. Please check your local retailers to find these materials, or go to a company's Web site for the latest product. In addition, we have made every attempt to properly credit the items mentioned in this book. We apologize to any company that we have listed incorrectly, and we would appreciate hearing from you.

An (*) has been placed next to the names of companies who donated products toward the creation of the artwork in this book.

3L Corporation
(800) 828-3130
www.scrapbook-adhesives.com

3M
(800) 364-3577
www.3m.com

7gypsies
(877) 749-7797
www.sevengypsies.com

A2Z Essentials
(419) 663-2869
www.geta2z.com

Ad Tech/Adhesive Technologies, Inc.
(800) 458-3486
www.adhesivetech.com

Adobe Systems Incorporated
(800) 833-6687
www.adobe.com

Adornit/Carolee's Creations*
(435) 563-1100
www.adornit.com

Aleene's - see Duncan

All My Memories
(888) 553-1998
www.allmymemories.com

American Crafts*
(801) 226-0747
www.americancrafts.com

American Traditional Designs
(800) 448-6656
www.americantraditional.com

ANW Crestwood
(973) 406-5000
www.anwcrestwood.com

Anna Griffin, Inc.
(888) 817-8170
www.annagriffin.com

Arctic Frog*
(479) 636-3764
www.arcticfrog.com

Around The Block
(801) 593-1946
www.aroundtheblockproducts.com

Art Declassified*
www.artdeclassified.com

Autumn Leaves
(800) 588-6707
www.autumnleaves.com

Avery Dennison Corporation
(800) 462-8379
www.avery.com

BasicGrey*
(801) 544-1116
www.basicgrey.com

Bazzill Basics Paper*
(480) 558-8557
www.bazzillbasics.com

Beacon Adhesives
(914) 699-3405
www.beaconcreates.com

Beary Patch Inc.
(877) 327-2111
www.bearypatchinc.com

Berwick Offray, LLC
(800) 344-5533
www.offray.com

Board Dudes, Inc.
(951) 808-9347
www.boarddudes.com

Bo-Bunny Press*
(801) 771-4010
www.bobunny.com

Cactus Pink*
(866) 798-2446
www.cactuspink.com

Canson, Inc.
(800) 628-9283
www.canson-us.com

Chatterbox, Inc.
(888) 416-6260
www.chatterboxinc.com

CherryArte*
(212) 465-3495
www.cherryarte.com

Clearsnap, Inc.
(888) 448-4862
www.clearsnap.com

Cloud 9 Design*
(866) 348-5661
www.cloud9design.biz

Collage Press
(435) 676-2039
www.collagepress.com

Cosmo Cricket*
(800) 852-8810
www.cosmocricket.com

Crate Paper*
(801) 798-8996
www.cratepaper.com

Creative Imaginations
(800) 942-6487
www.cigift.com

Creative Memories
(800) 468-9335
www.creativememories.com

Daisy Bucket Designs*
(541) 289-3299
www.daisybucketdesigns.com

Daisy D's Paper Company*
(888) 601-8955
www.daisydspaper.com

Darice, Inc.
(800) 321-1494
www.darice.com

DecoArt Inc.
(800) 367-3047
www.decoart.com

Dèjá Views
(800) 243-8419
www.dejaviews.com

Delish Designs*
(360) 897-1254
www.delishdesigns.com

Delta Technical Coatings, Inc.
(800) 423-4135
www.deltacrafts.com

Designer Digitals
www.designerdigitals.com

Dick Blick Holdings, Inc.
(800) 828-4548
www.dickblick.com

Die Cuts With A View*
(801) 224-6766
www.diecutswithaview.com

DMC Corp.
(973) 589-0606
www.dmc-usa.com

Doodlebug Design Inc.
(877) 800-9190
www.doodlebug.ws

Dream Street Papers*
(480) 275-9736
www.dreamstreetpapers.com

Dress It Up
www.dressitup.com

Duncan Enterprises
(800) 438-6226
www.duncanceramics.com

Dymo
(800) 426-7827
www.dymo.com

Ebay
www.ebay.com

EK Success, Ltd.
(800) 524-1349
www.eksuccess.com

Emagination Crafts, Inc.
(866) 238-9770
www.emaginationcrafts.com

Fancy Pants Designs, LLC*
(801) 779-3212
www.fancypantsdesigns.com

Fibre-Craft Materials Corp.
(847) 647-1140
www.fibrecraft.com

Fiskars, Inc.*
(866) 348-5661
www.fiskars.com

Flair Designs*
(888) 546-9990
www.flairdesignsinc.com

Fontwerks
(604) 942-3105
www.fontwerks.com

Gel-à-tins*
(800) 393-2151
www.gelatinstamps.com

Glue Dots International
(888) 688-7131
www.gluedots.com

Go West Studios
(214) 227-0007
www.goweststudios.com

Golden Artist Colors, Inc.
(800) 959-6543
www.goldenpaints.com

Gymboree Corporation
www.gymboree.com

Hallmark Cards, Inc.
(800) 425-5627
www.hallmark.com

Hambly Studios
(800) 451-3999
www.hamblystudios.com

Hammermill - see International Paper Company

Heidi Grace Designs, Inc.*
(866) 348-5661
www.heidigrace.com

Heidi Swapp/Advantus Corporation*
(904) 482-0092
www.heidiswapp.com

Henkel Consumer Adhesives, Inc.
(800) 321-0253
www.stickwithhenkel.com

Herma GmbH
www.herma.com

Imagination Project, Inc.*
(888) 477-6532
www.imaginationproject.com

Imaginisce*
(801) 908-8111
www.imaginisce.com

Jen Wilson Designs
www.jenwilsondesigns.com

Jo-Ann Stores
www.joann.com

Junkitz*
(732) 792-1108
www.junkitz.com

K&Company*
(888) 244-2083
www.kandcompany.com

Karen Foster Design
(801) 451-9779
www.karenfosterdesign.com

KI Memories
(972) 243-5595
www.kimemories.com

Lasting Impressions for Paper, Inc.
(800) 936-2677
www.lastingimpressions.com

Li'l Davis Designs
(480) 223-0080
www.lildavisdesigns.com

L'Orna/Kandi Corp.
(800) 985-2634
www.l-orna.com

Magic Scraps
(904) 482-0092
www.magicscraps.com

Magistical Memories
(818) 842-1540
www.magisticalmemories.com

Making Memories*
(801) 294-0430
www.makingmemories.com

Martha Stewart Crafts/Delivery Agent, Inc.
www.marthastewartcrafts.com

Marvy Uchida/ Uchida of America, Corp.
(800) 541-5877
www.uchida.com

May Arts
(800) 442-3950
www.mayarts.com

Maya Road, LLC
(214) 488-3279
www.mayaroad.com

me & my BiG ideas
(949) 583-2065
www.meandmybigideas.com

Melissa Frances/Heart & Home, Inc.*
(888) 616-6166
www.melissafrances.com

Memories Complete, LLC
(866) 966-6365
www.memoriescomplete.com

Michaels Arts & Crafts
(800) 642-4235
www.michaels.com

Microsoft Corporation
www.microsoft.com

Mill Hill
www.millhill.com

Mustard Moon*
(763) 493-5157
www.mustardmoon.com

My Little Shoebox, LLC*
(510) 269-4162
www.mylittleshoebox.com

My Mind's Eye, Inc.
(800) 665-5116
www.mymindseye.com

Offray- see Berwick Offray, LLC

One Heart...One Mind, LLC*
(888) 414-3690

Paper Company, The - see ANW Crestwood

Paper Salon*
(800) 627-2648
www.papersalon.com

Pebbles Inc.
(801) 235-1520
www.pebblesinc.com

Piggy Tales*
(702) 755-8600
www.piggytales.com

Plaid Enterprises, Inc.
(800) 842-4197
www.plaidonline.com

Polar Bear Press
(801) 451-7670
www.polarbearpress.com

Pressed Petals*
(800) 748-4656
www.pressedpetals.com

Prima Marketing, Inc.*
(909) 627-5532
www.primamarketinginc.com

Prism Papers
(866) 902-1002
www.prismpapers.com

Provo Craft
(800) 937-7686
www.provocraft.com

Purple Onion Designs*
www.purpleoniondesigns.com

Queen & Co.
(858) 613-7858
www.queenandcompany.com

QuicKutz, Inc.
(888) 702-1146
www.quickutz.com

Ranger Industries, Inc.*
(800) 244-2211
www.rangerink.com

Reminisce Papers
(319) 358-9777
www.shopreminisce.com

Robin's Nest Press, The
(435) 789-5387
robins@sbnet.com

Rouge de Garance*
www.rougedegarance.com

Rusty Pickle
(801) 746-1045
www.rustypickle.com

Sakura Hobby Craft
(310) 212-7878
www.sakuracraft.com

Sandylion Sticker Designs
(800) 387-4215
www.sandylion.com

Sanford Corporation
(800) 323-0749
www.sanfordcorp.com

Sassafras Lass
(801) 269-1331
www.sassafraslass.com

Savvy Stamps
(866) 447-2889
www.savvystamps.com

Scenic Route Paper Co.
(801) 225-5754
www.scenicroutepaper.com

ScrapArtist
(734) 717-7775
www.scrapartist.com

Scrapworks, LLC / As You Wish Products, LLC
(801) 363-1010
www.scrapworks.com

Scribble Scrabble LLC*
(801) 400-9741
www.scribblescrabble.net

SEI, Inc.
(800) 333-3279
www.shopsei.com

Sharpie - see Sanford

Shoebox Trims
(303) 257-7578
www.shoeboxtrims.com

Sideshow Stamps
www.sideshowstamps.com

Sizzix
(877) 355-4766
www.sizzix.com

Stampin' Up!
(800) 782-6787
www.stampinup.com

Stamps by Judith
www.stampsbyjudith.com

StazOn - see Tsukineko

Stemma/Masterpiece Studios*
www.masterpiecestudios.com

Strano Designs
(508) 454-4615
www.stranodesigns.com

Sugarloaf Products, Inc.
(770) 484-0722
www.sugarloafproducts.com

Sweetwater
(800) 359-3094
www.sweetwaterscrapbook.com

Technique Tuesday, LLC
(503) 644-4073
www.techniquetuesday.com

Therm O Web, Inc.
(800) 323-0799
www.thermoweb.com

Three Bugs in a Rug, LLC*
(801) 804-6657
www.threebugsinarug.com

Time Flies Design
(845) 726-3646
www.timefliesdesign.net

Tinkering Ink*
(877) 727-2784
www.tinkeringink.com

Tombow
(800) 835-3232
www.tombowusa.com

Tsukineko, Inc.
(800) 769-6633
www.tsukineko.com

Two Peas in a Bucket
(888) 896-7327
www.twopeasinabucket.com

Upsy Daisy Designs*
www.upsydaisydesigns.com

Urban Lily*
www.urbanlily.com

VersaMark - see Tsukineko

We R Memory Keepers, Inc.
(801) 539-5000
www.weronthenet.com

Weavewerks
www.weavewerks.com

Webster's Pages/Webster Fine Art Limited
(800) 543-6104
www.websterspages.com

WorldWin Papers
(888) 834-6455
www.worldwinpapers.com

Wrights Ribbon Accents
(877) 597-4448
www.wrights.com

Wübie Prints*
(888) 256-0107
www.wubieprints.com

Xyron
(800) 793-3523
www.xyron.com

Zsiage, LLC
(718) 224-1976
www.zsiage.com

index

Discover more innovative ideas and page design tips with these Memory Makers Books!

Flip, Spin & Play

Step-by-step instructions on a variety of techniques show you how to create engaging, interactive pages that beg to be touched.

ISBN-10: 1-59963-018-4
ISBN-13: 978-1-59963-018-2
paperback
128 pages
Z1679

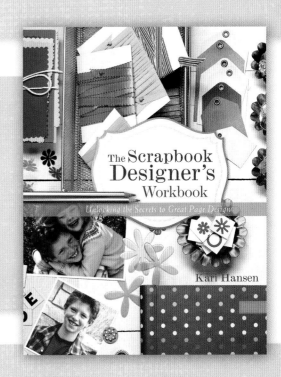

The Scrapbook Designer's Workbook

Join author Kari Hansen as she takes the fear out of understanding and using design principles to create fabulous scrapbook layouts.

ISBN-13: 978-1-892127-95-2
ISBN-10: 1-892127-95-4
hardcover with enclosed spiral
128 pages
Z0533

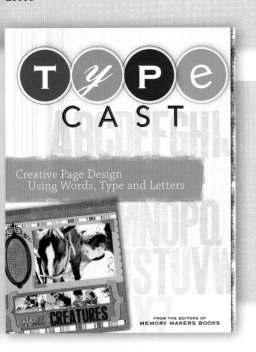

Type Cast

Learn fresh, creative uses for a variety of type treatments as well as expert tips on composing attention-getting titles and getting into the flow of journaling.

ISBN-13: 978-59963-003-8
ISBN-10: 1-59963-003-6
paperback
128 pages
Z0695

These books and other fine Memory Makers titles are available at your local scrapbook or craft retailer, bookstore or from online suppliers. And check out our Web site at www.memorymakersmagazine.com.

scrapbook
page|maps

CardAssemblyInstructions

In the following section, you will find 60 bonus cards with the sketches featured in the book. Included on the backside of each card is a sample layout and a short list of supplies I recommend. These cards are handy when shopping for supplies or for cropping-on-the-go. All you have to do is tuck your favorite sketches into your purse or crop bag and off you go!

To create the box, follow these simple instructions.

Punch out the box along the perforated lines.

Fold along crease lines and secure the length-wise open end with adhesive or transparent tape.

Fold the remaining pieces in place, and voilà! All 60 cards will fit easily into the box. Decorate the outside of the box if desired.

12 x 12 single

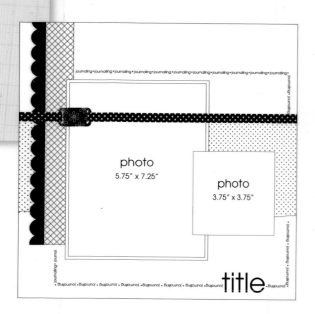

photo
5.75" x 7.25"

photo
3.75" x 3.75"

journaling • journaling • journaling • journaling • journaling • journaling • journaling •

title

2-photo sketch on page 10

12 x 12 single

photo
6" x 4"

photo

photo
6" x 4"

title

3-photo sketch on page 12

8½ x 11 horizontal

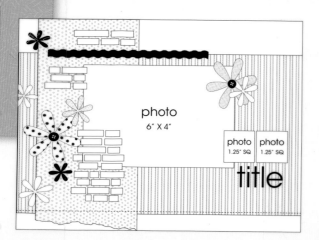

photo
6" X 4"

photo
1.25" SQ

photo
1.25" SQ

title

3-photo sketch on page 13

12 x 12 double

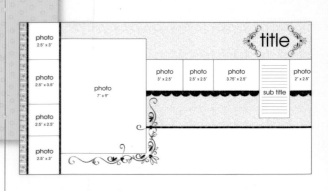

photo
2.5" x 3"

photo
2.5" x 3.5"

photo
2.5" x 2.5"

photo
2.5" x 3"

photo
7" x 9"

title

photo
3" x 2.5"

photo
2.5" 2.5"

photo
3.75" x 2.5"

sub title

photo
2" x 2.5"

9-photo sketch on page 15

Art created by **Becky Fleck**

Materials to try:

- Buttons
- Large grommets
- Felt flowers

Art created by **Becky Fleck**

Materials to try:

- Chipboard flower
- Large rub-ons for title
- Eyelets

Art created by **Becky Fleck**

Materials to try:

- Felt embellishments
- Foam letters
- Chipboard circles

Art created by **Marla Kress**

Materials to try:

- Patterned paper cut-outs
- Chipboard letters
- Clear flowers

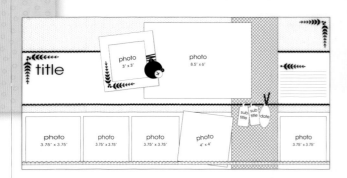

title

photo
3" x 3"

photo
8.5" x 6"

sub
title

sub
title

date

photo
3.75" x 3.75"

photo
3.75" x 3.75"

photo
3.75" x 3.75"

photo
4" x 4"

photo
3.75" x 3.75"

7-photo sketch on page **25**

photo
6" x 4"

title

photo
3.25" x 3.25"

photo
3.25" x 3.25"

3-photo sketch on page **26**

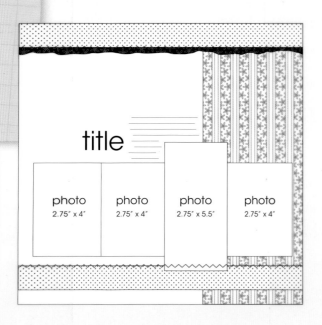

title

photo
2.75" x 4"

photo
2.75" x 4"

photo
2.75" x 5.5"

photo
2.75" x 4"

4-photo sketch on page **29**

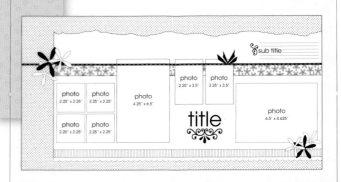

sub title

photo
2.25" x 2.25"

photo
2.25" x 2.25"

photo
4.25" x 6.5"

photo
2.25" x 3.5"

photo
2.25" x 3.5"

photo
2.25" x 2.25"

photo
2.25" x 2.25"

title

photo
6.5" x 4.625"

8-photo sketch on page **31**

12 x 12 single

tickled pink doesn't adequately describe how delighted you were with the two pink flamingos we gave you for your flower garden! They were such an impulsive gift on my part, and yet they thrilled you more than anything else on your birthday. It's awesome that something as simple as two silly flamingos brightened your day. Those funky birds do kind of look like us when we go shopping, don't they?!

pink

Art created by **Becky Fleck**

Materials to try:
- Library card for journaling
- Rub-on letters
- Acrylic letters

12 x 12 double

Art created by **Becky Fleck**

Materials to try:
- Sticker shapes
- Chipboard letters
- Rub-on flourishes

12 x 12 double

Hollandia Nursery

Art created by **Becky Fleck**

Materials to try:
- Silk flowers
- Transparency overlays
- Epoxy tags

12 x 12 single

You are almost a year old now! I can't believe how quickly the time has passed! You bring us so much joy and we love to see that cute little smile of yours. We get this grin every single day, sweet, happy and always with your tongue sticking out!

tongue

Art created by **Mindy Bush**

Materials to try:
- Plastic letters
- Chipboard letters
- Machine stitching

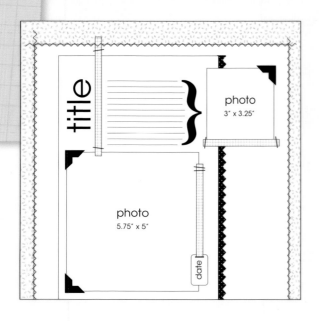

title

photo
3" x 3.25"

photo
5.75" x 5"

date

2-photo sketch on page **32**

title

photo
6" x 6"

photo
2.25" x 3"

photo
2.25" x 2.25"

3-photo sketch on page **33**

title

date

photo
2.5" x 2.5"

photo
4" x 6.75"

2-photo sketch on page **35**

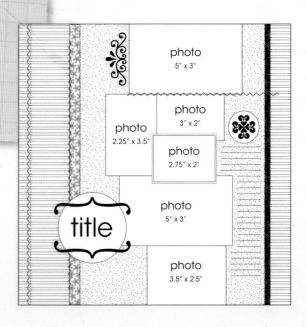

photo
5" x 3"

photo
3" x 2"

photo
2.25" x 3.5"

photo
2.75" x 2"

photo
5" x 3"

title

photo
3.5" x 2.5"

6-photo sketch on page **36**

Art created by **Becky Fleck**

Materials to try:

- Foam embellishments
- Letter stickers
- Pre-printed quotes

Art created by **Becky Fleck**

Materials to try:

- Acrylic letters
- Rub-on brackets
- Stamps

Art created by **Becky Fleck**

Materials to try:

- Fabric ribbon
- Stamped flourish
- Machine sewing

Art created by **Marla Kress**

Materials to try:

- Jumbo buttons or brads
- Pre-printed chipboard title
- Rub-on stitches

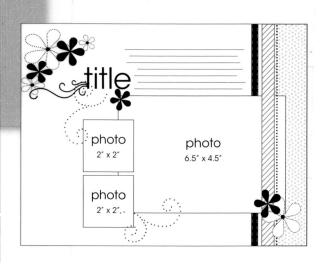

title

photo
2″ x 2″

photo
2″ x 2″

photo
6.5″ x 4.5″

3-photo sketch on page **40**

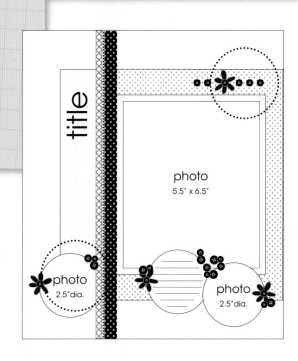

title

photo
5.5″ x 6.5″

photo
2.5″ dia.

photo
2.5″ dia.

3-photo sketch on page **42**

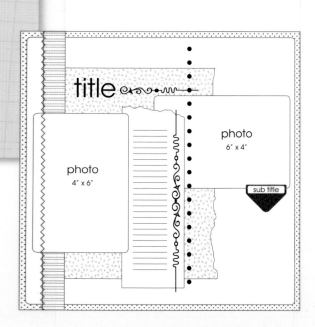

title

photo
4″ x 6″

photo
6″ x 4″

sub title

2-photo sketch on page **44**

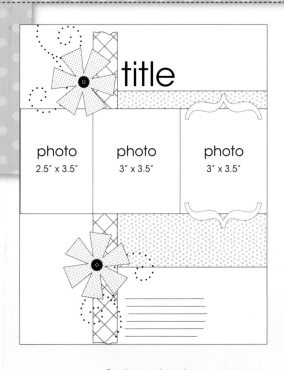

title

photo
2.5″ x 3.5″

photo
3″ x 3.5″

photo
3″ x 3.5″

3-photo sketch on page **45**

Art created by **Becky Fleck**

Materials to try:

• Rhinestones

• Letter stickers

• Paper flowers

Art created by **Denine Zielinski**

Materials to try:

• Felt embellishments

• Flourish stamps

• Epoxy stickers

Art created by **Becky Fleck**

Materials to try:

• Chipboard flourishes

• Plastic brackets

• Rub-on flourishes

Art created by **Becky Fleck**

Materials to try:

• Chipboard letters

• Buttons

• Rub-on stitches

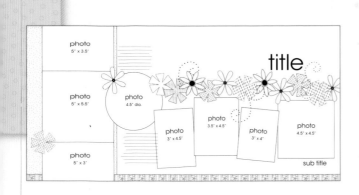

photo
5˝ x 3.5˝

photo
5˝ x 5.5˝

photo
4.5˝ dia.

photo
3˝ x 4.5˝

photo
3.5˝ x 4.5˝

photo
3˝ x 4˝

photo
4.5˝ x 4.5˝

title

sub title

photo
5˝ x 3˝

photo
8˝ x 4.5˝

title

photo
3.5˝ x 2.25˝

8-photo sketch on page **47**

2-photo sketch on page **48**

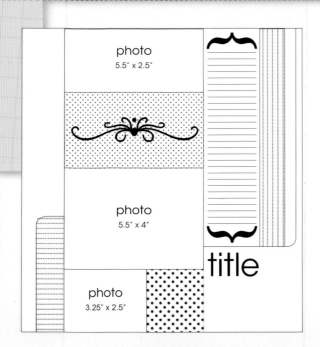

photo
5.5˝ x 2.5˝

photo
5.5˝ x 4˝

title

photo
3.25˝ x 2.5˝

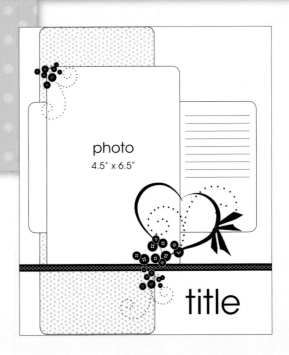

photo
4.5˝ x 6.5˝

title

3-photo sketch on page **50**

1-photo sketch on page **52**

Art created by **Denine Zielinski**

Materials to try:
- Foam flowers
- Flourish stamps
- Pre-printed mini tags

Art created by **Marla Kress**

Materials to try:
- Die-cut stars
- Rub-ons letters
- Journaling

Art created by **Becky Fleck**

Materials to try:
- Rub-on designs
- Felt trim
- Foam letter stickers

Art created by **Becky Fleck**

Materials to try:
- Chipboard heart
- Fabric brads
- Sequins or rhinestones

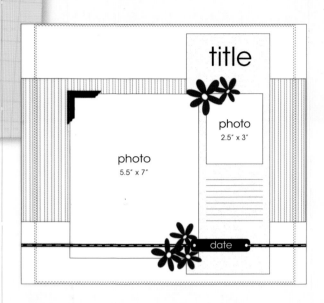

title

photo
2.5˝ x 3˝

photo
5.5˝ x 7˝

date

2-photo sketch on page **54**

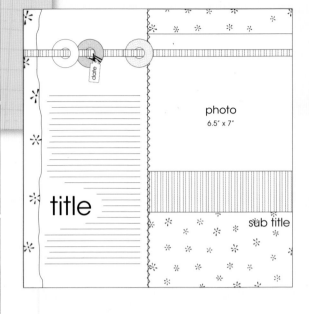

date

photo
6.5˝ x 7˝

title

sub title

1-photo sketch on page **56**

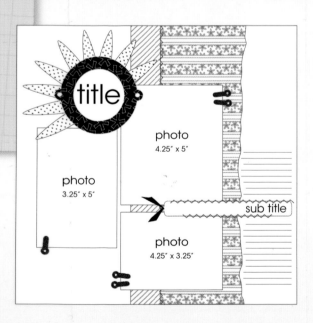

title

photo
4.25˝ x 5˝

photo
3.25˝ x 5˝

sub title

photo
4.25˝ x 3.25˝

3-photo sketch on page **57**

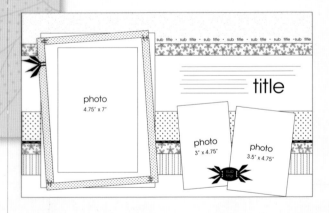

sub title · sub title · sub title · sub title · sub title · sub title · sub title

photo
4.75˝ x 7˝

title

photo
3˝ x 4.75˝

photo
3.5˝ x 4.75˝

3-photo sketch on page **58**

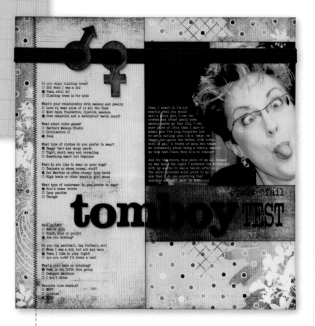

Art created by **Becky Fleck**

Materials to try:
- Acrylic washers
- Rickrack
- Chipboard letters

Art created by **Becky Fleck**

Materials to try:
- Paper flowers
- Mini brads
- Letter stickers

Art created by **Becky Fleck**

Materials to try:
- Acrylic letters
- Pre-cut frame
- Die-cut index tabs

Art created by **Becky Fleck**

Materials to try:
- Die-cut strips
- Mini metal tags
- Rub-on letters

12 x 12 single

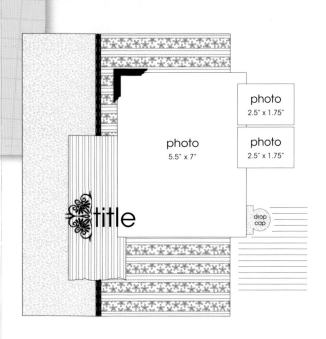

3-photo sketch on page **60**

12 x 12 double

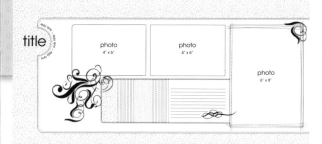

3-photo sketch on page **63**

12 x 12 single

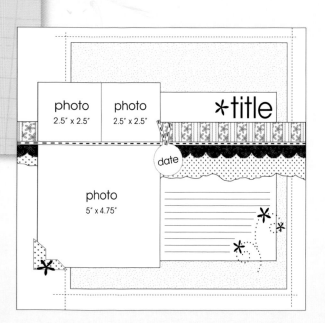

3-photo sketch on page **64**

12 x 12 single

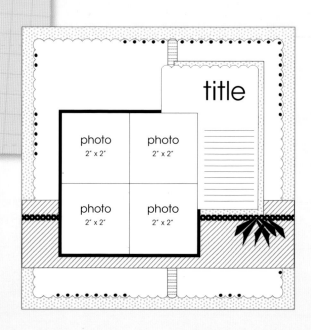

4-photo sketch on page **66**

12 x 12 double

Art created by **Becky Fleck**

Materials to try:
- Seashells
- Epoxy stickers
- Rub-on designs

12 x 12 single

Art created by **Becky Fleck**

Materials to try:
- Sticker borders
- Buttons
- Chipboard letters

12 x 12 single

Art created by **Tiffany Tillman**

Materials to try:
- Acrylic letters
- Felt embellishments
- Epoxy brads

12 x 12 single

Art created by **Becky Fleck**

Materials to try:
- Chipboard letters
- Rub-on stitches
- Sequins

12 x 12 double

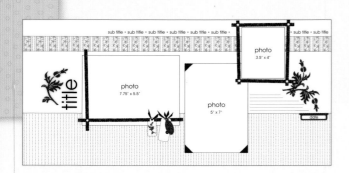

3-photo sketch on page **68**

12 x 12 single

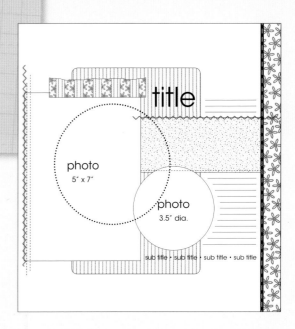

2-photo sketch on page **72**

8½ x 11 horizontal

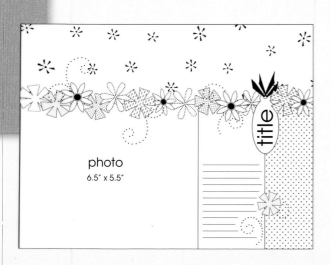

1-photo sketch on page **74**

12 x 12 single

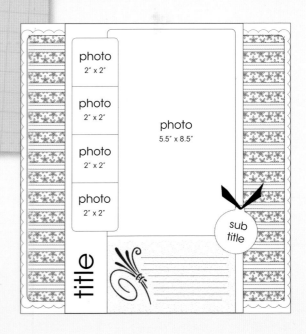

5-photo sketch on page **76**

12 x 12 single

Art created by **Tiffany Tillman**

Materials to try:
• Transparency overlay
• Decorative scissors
• Large rub-on letters

12 x 12 double

Art created by **Becky Fleck**

Materials to try:
• Foam shapes
• Pre-made frame
• Rhinestones

12 x 12 single

Art created by **Becky Fleck**

Materials to try:
• Epoxy stickers
• Large buttons or brads
• Die-cut letters

8½ x 11 horizontal

Art created by **Patti Milazzo**

Materials to try:
• Journaling tags
• Letter stamps
• Rub-on stitches

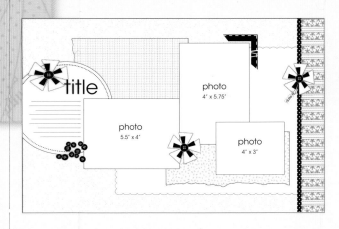

title

photo
4" x 5.75"

photo
5.5" x 4"

photo
4" x 3"

3-photo sketch on page **78**

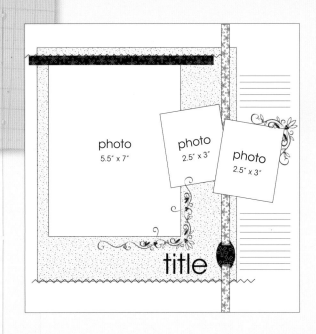

photo
5.5" x 7"

photo
2.5" x 3"

photo
2.5" x 3"

title

3-photo sketch on page **80**

date

photo
6.25" x 7.75"

sub title

*title

1-photo sketch on page **82**

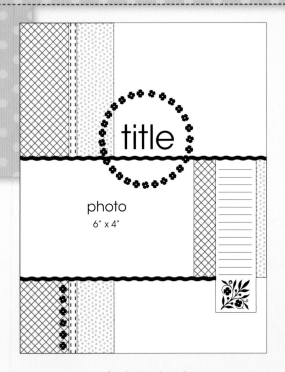

title

photo
6" x 4"

1-photo sketch on page **85**

12 x 12 single

Art created by **Mindy Bush**

Materials to try:
- Designer stamps
- Foam letters
- Label maker

8½ x 11 double

Art created by **Sheredian Vickers**

Materials to try:
- Silk flowers
- Jumbo brads
- Rub-on letters

8½ x 11 vertical

Art created by **Judi VanValkinburgh**

Materials to try:
- Felt flowers
- Pre-cut borders
- Journaling stamp

12 x 12 single

Art created by **Marla Kress**

Materials to try:
- Metal rim tag
- Epoxy stickers
- Acrylic bookplate

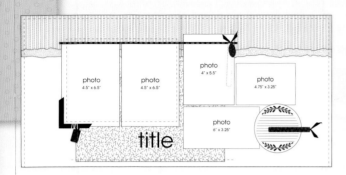

5-photo sketch on page **87**

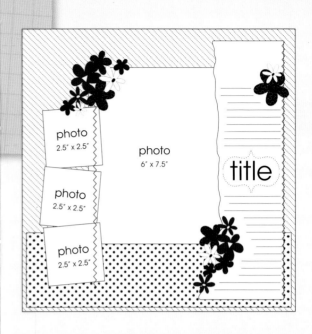

4-photo sketch on page **88**

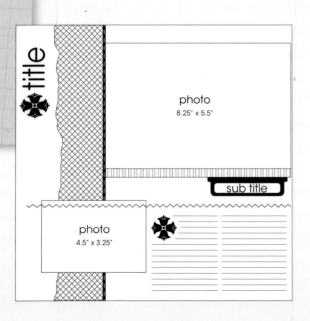

2-photo sketch on page **90**

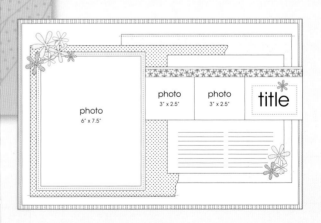

3-photo sketch on page **94**

Art created by **Becky Fleck**

Materials to try:
- Rickrack
- Foam embellishments
- Letter stamps

Art created by **Marla Kress**

Materials to try:
- Digital elements
- Chipboard stars
- Rub-on flourishes

Art created by **Denine Zielinski**

Materials to try:
- Felt flowers
- Lace paper
- Fabric

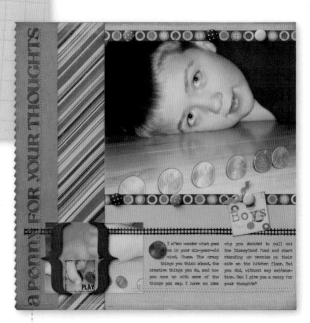

Art created by **Becky Fleck**

Materials to try:
- Photo turns
- Chipboard brackets
- Rub-on letters

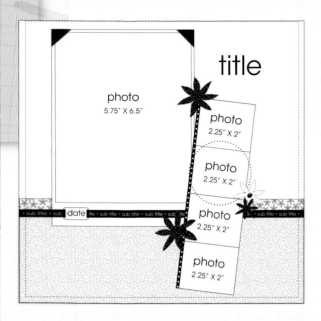

title

photo
5.75" X 6.5"

photo
2.25" X 2"

photo
2.25" x 2"

photo
2.25" X 2"

photo
2.25" X 2"

· sub title · sub: date title · sub title · sub title · sub · fle · sub title · sub title ·

5-photo sketch on page **96**

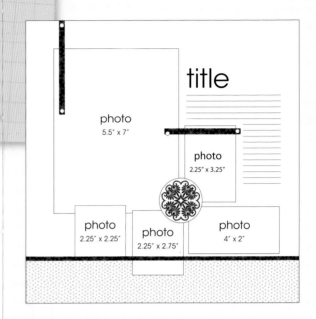

title

photo
5.5" x 7"

photo
2.25" x 3.25"

photo
2.25" x 2.25"

photo
2.25" x 2.75"

photo
4" x 2"

5-photo sketch on page **97**

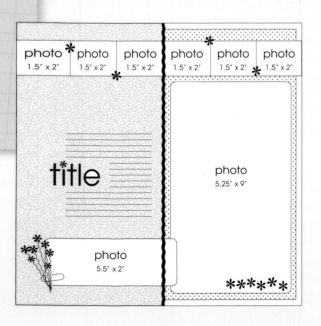

photo
1.5" x 2"

photo
1.5" x 2"

photo
1.5" x 2"

photo
1.5" x 2"

photo
1.5" x 2"

photo
1.5" x 2"

title

photo
5.25" x 9"

photo
5.5" x 2"

*****

8-photo sketch on page **99**

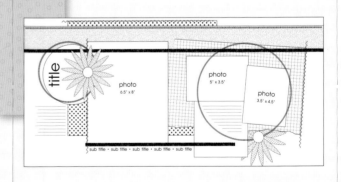

title

photo
6.5" x 8"

photo
5" x 3.5"

photo
3.5" x 4.5"

· sub title · sub title · sub title · sub title · sub title ·

3-photo sketch on page **101**

Art created by **Becky Fleck**

Materials to try:
- Large silk flower
- Small buttons
- Letter stickers

Art created by **Becky Fleck**

Materials to try:
- Brads
- Rub-on flourishes
- Chipboard letters

Art created by **Marla Kress**

Materials to try:
- Acrylic letters
- Paper flowers
- Word stickers

Art created by **Judi VanValkinburgh**

Materials to try:
- Felt letters
- Epoxy stickers
- Photo turns

photo
1.25˝ dia.

photo
4.5˝ x 5.5˝

title

2-photo sketch on page **102**

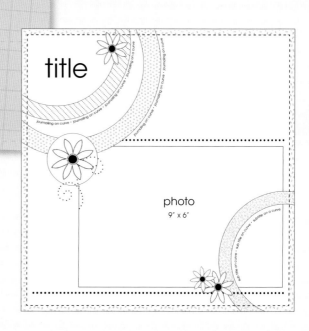

title

photo
9˝ x 6˝

1-photo sketch on page **103**

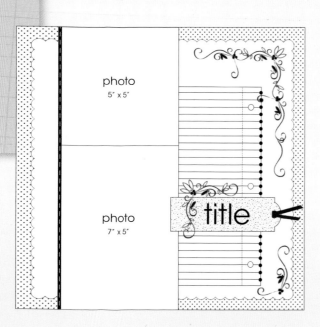

photo
5˝ x 5˝

photo
7˝ x 5˝

title

2-photo sketch on page **104**

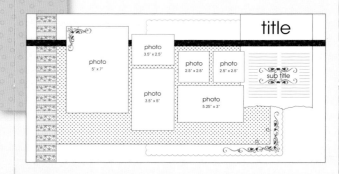

title

photo
5˝ x 7˝

photo
3.5˝ x 2.5˝

photo
2.5˝ x 2.5˝

photo
2.5˝ x 2.5˝

photo
3.5˝ x 5˝

photo
5.25˝ x 3˝

sub title

6-photo sketch on page **107**

12 x 12 single

Art created by **Becky Fleck**

Materials to try:
- Letter stickers
- Felt shapes
- Large buttons

8½ x 11 vertical

Art created by **Becky Fleck**

Materials to try:
- Silk flower
- Rub-on designs
- Letter stickers

12 x 12 double

Art created by **Tiffany Tillman**

Materials to try:
- Acrylic letters
- Stamp designs
- Chipboard frames

12 x 12 single

Art created by **Denine Zielinski**

Materials to try:
- Foam letters
- Rhinestones
- Sticker border

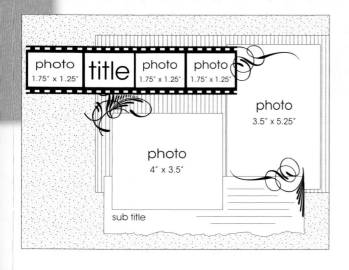

photo
1.75" x 1.25"

title

photo
1.75" x 1.25"

photo
1.75" x 1.25"

photo
3.5" x 5.25"

photo
4" x 3.5"

sub title

5-photo sketch on page **108**

photo
6.5" x 5.5"

photo
3" x 4"

photo
3" x 4"

title

3-photo sketch on page **110**

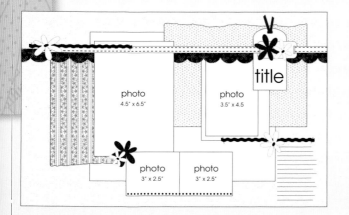

title

photo
4.5" x 6.5"

photo
3.5" x 4.5

photo
3" x 2.5"

photo
3" x 2.5"

4-photo sketch on page **112**

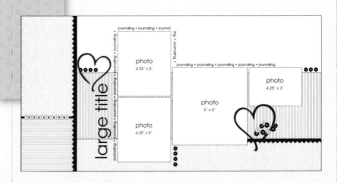

journaling • journaling • journal

photo
4.25" x 5"

journaling • journaling • journaling • journaling • journaling

photo
4.25" x 3"

large title

photo
6" x 6"

photo
4.25" x 5"

4-photo sketch on page **114**

Art created by **Becky Fleck**

Materials to try:

- Felt shapes
- Journaling tag
- Rub-on letters

Art created by **Marla Kress**

Materials to try:

- Transparency frame
- Chipboard letters
- Designer stickers

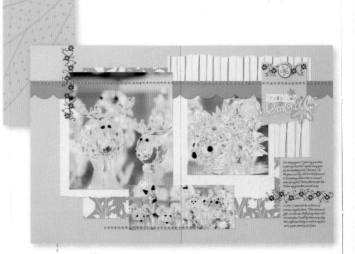

Art created by **Becky Fleck**

Materials to try:

- Jumbo brads
- Rub-on stitches
- Letter stickers

Art created by **Becky Fleck**

Materials to try:

- Mini brads
- Rub-on flourishes
- Acrylic frame

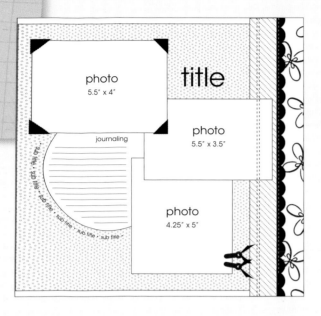

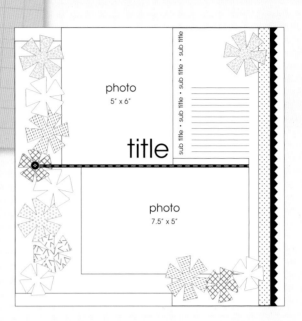

3-photo sketch on page 116

2-photo sketch on page 117

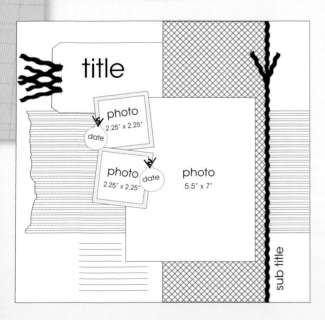

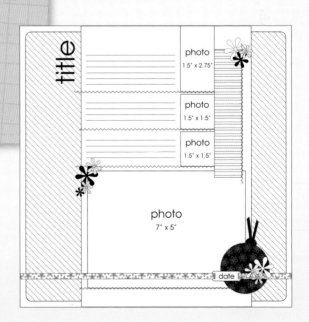

3-photo sketch on page 118

4-photo sketch on page 119

Art created by **Denine Zielinski**

Materials to try:

- Jumbo brads
- Chipboard letters
- Die-cut border

Art created by **Becky Fleck**

Materials to try:

- Foam shapes
- Rub-on letters
- Rhinestones

Art created by **Becky Fleck**

Materials to try:

- Letter stickers
- Journaling tags
- Word stickers

Art created by **Mindy Bush**

Materials to try:

- Foam flowers
- Decorative scissors
- Rub-on letters